God, Why Am I Sick?

Seven Biblical Reasons Why People Get Sick

PAUL and CAROLYN WILDE

**All Scripture quotations are taken from the
King James version of the Bible.**

Excerpt from the song, **Jesus Use Me**, by Billy and Jack Campbell.
© Copyright 1956 by Gospel Publishing House. Arr. Copyright
1963 by Gospel Publishing House in Melody Choruses. All rights
reserved. Used by Permission.

A WORD FROM CAROLYN ...

Although I was the one who penned the words of this book, I could not omit Paul's name, as co-author.

Paul is a preacher. I have listened to him preach thousands of anointed sermons from the Bible. We spend countless hours and entire days together, discussing the inexhaustible riches of God's Word.

Our ideas blend, our thoughts become one, and our desire to proclaim the Word of God is shared. We discuss every word of a book, before publishing it. Paul is constantly telling me: "Simplify that sentence! Make it plain!"

(Many, who have heard him preach, say: "He was talking right to me – and I knew exactly what he was saying! He makes the Word so plain!")

So, I do as he says, and people generally say the same thing about my books!

We both pray that **"God, Why Am I Sick?"** will be a blessing, encouragement, and help to you.

PAUL AND CAROLYN WILDE
401 W. MARIGOLD AVENUE
FOLEY, ALABAMA 36535
TELEPHONE: (251) 949-7771
EMAIL: PCWILDE@GULFTEL.COM

COMMENTS FROM READERS

"I am a 22 year old girl. I was given your book as I lay on my hospital bed, facing a critical surgery. I read the seven reasons for sickness, and I discovered my reason! I prayed the prayer given at the end of the chapter dealing with my problem, and God gave me peace."

"Thank you for your book on sickness! No book, other than the Bible, has helped me so much. My husband, a faithful pastor for years, has suffered a devastating stroke. I have finally found answers to my many questions, and my faith in a loving God has been restored."

"My life has been transformed by the Scriptural truths in your book on sickness! My body was failing fast, and I could hardly walk or move my hands. Then I discovered faith for a miracle – and received mine! I am 81 years old, and God, in His mercy, has healed my body and renewed my strength! I am praising my Healer, serving Him daily, visiting and singing to those younger than I in nursing homes – and even playing golf again!"

"My wonderful husband lies paralyzed from a recent stroke. I read your book aloud to him, as I lay beside his helpless body. We have prayed the prayer for salvation together. God has given us the greatest miracle Gift of all, in the Person of His Son, now our personal Savior."

"I am 34 years old. My doctors have pronounced the dreaded sentence, Cancer. I have found the answer to my question, God, why am I sick, through the Scriptures quoted in your book."

"This book is so needed for our day, and is a good book to give out in a hospital. It is very well-balanced and gives hope. God's love is clearly seen throughout the book."

FOREWORD

Both Carolyn and Paul Wilde, husband and wife, are two of the most talented disciples of Jesus Christ that I have had the privilege of knowing.

At first, I was attracted to their ministry by their musical abilities. Then I was made aware of the width and depth of their multifarious service to the community; not only in the consistency of their emphasis on the saving power of the gospel, but also on their practical social efforts to feed and clothe those in need in their immediate geographical area. Then, over and beyond these commendable avenues of service, they engage in a special ministry under the caption of "Smitten Shepherds." They had obtained and furnished two houses and dedicated them as temporary places of refuge for pastors and their families who had suffered various wounds from the spiritual warfare in which they had been engaged.

However, most of all, my admiration for Carolyn and Paul Wilde is evident in the content of this present book. As in Carolyn's adult Sunday School classes, and in Paul's pulpit messages, their teaching and preaching are chock-a-block full of references from Holy Scripture.

I have read many books on the mystery and the ministry of sickness and suffering, but I have yet to find one that can compare with their book. Not only does the work stretch the mind, but it touches the heart by its use of Holy Spirit inspired truth.

Many believers have found help and enlightenment in the ministries of the Wilde's, and I am confident that many more will continue to do so, especially as they interact with the truths that echo throughout this book. My prayer is that such might be the case, and that consequently they may continue to grow in that quality of life that truly honors and glorifies the Savior, the Lord Jesus Christ.

Pastor Henry T. Hudson (BA, MA, MTh, DD.)

CONTENTS

Dear Reader:

You no doubt know people who have had a terminal sickness, and in their desperation, have reached out to God for a miracle. We know some who have received a death-defying miracle that could only be explained by a divine touch from God.

Then we have known others, who have reached out to God for their miracle, but the miracle they prayed for did not come. Instead of a touch from God, that they had pleaded for, they were left with confusion, turmoil — and their sickness. Why did they remain sick, while others were healed? Was God angry with them? Were they lacking faith? Did God not love them? Were their prayers even heard by God? Where was this loving God when they needed Him?

Controversy rages today, and the sick who need help the most are caught in the conflict of teachings.

"All sickness comes from the devil!"

"The day of miracles is over!"

"If you had faith, you would not be sick in the first place!"

The sickness is bad enough. But the spiritual frustration is nearly as bad, if not even worse! This book is dedicated to you, who are sick and searching for an answer during your time of crisis.

If you are sick, the question perhaps keeps repeating itself in your mind: "Why me, God? Why have You let this happen to me?"

It was God's Son, Jesus, who said, "Ask, and it shall be given you; seek, and ye shall find, knock, and it shall be opened unto you: for every one that asketh receiveth; and he that seeketh findeth; and to him that knocketh, it shall be opened." (Matthew 7:7-8)

Are you knocking at heaven's door, seeking admission to the throne room of God, so you can ask your Creator for His help? God made you. God is the only One who has all the answers to all of your questions. And God loves you enough to answer your questions. He has promised to those who meet His conditions: "... the peace of God, which passeth all understanding shall keep your hearts and minds through Christ Jesus." (Philippians 4:7)

It may have been a long time since you have had peace of heart and mind. Perhaps you have never had it. And maybe it is this nagging question that keeps you from having peace now: ***"God, why am I sick?"***

We have compiled seven Biblical reasons for sickness in this book. Some may not apply to you – but there may be one or more that will show you exactly why you are sick and how to deal with your sickness. Our prayer is that God will lead you personally to the reason that is especially for you.

We don't expect God to speak to you in an audible voice or appear at your bedside and point out the reason for your sickness – although He could. However, we do believe that if you study this book prayerfully and sincerely, when you read the chapter that is especially for you, God will put an assurance in your heart. You may then find yourself saying, "This is my answer."

The most important thing about your sickness is your attitude toward God.

Are you **angry** with Him for not keeping you healthy?

Are you **rebellious** toward Him? Do you feel as if He has no right to allow you to be sick – especially if you have been serving Him?

Are you **indifferent** toward Him? Have you decided that He really doesn't care whether you are sick or healthy? You may have even decided that since He doesn't care about you – why should you care about Him?

Are you **losing your faith and trust** in Him? After all, if He really loves you, is genuinely concerned about you, and has the capability to keep you healthy – why are you sick?

Are you **loving Him and trusting in His love and care** for you – even in your sickness?

Job cried from a pain-wracked body and a heart filled with agony: "Though he slay me, yet will I trust in Him!" (Job 13:15)

But that was Job. Are you able to repeat his words today … and mean them?

After studying the following pages, we pray all rebellion, anger, or indifference will be replaced with a strong, unshakable trust in your heavenly Father. He loves you. He knows what you are going through – and He cares.   Read the following prayer, and if you are able to pray it sincerely, do it right now, before starting this book.

"Dear God: You know I am sick. And You know that I want to know why You have allowed this to happen to me. If I am sick for a reason, and You want me to learn something through this sickness, please open up my heart to You. Remove any rebellion, anger, and unbelief that is in me.

"Help me to put myself into Your hands, and submit to Your will. Show me through the teaching of the Holy Spirit and the truths in Your Word, how I can grow closer to You – even through this sickness. I pray this in Jesus' name, who gave His life, so I can come to You for salvation, help, strength – and answers. Amen."

"*Ask, and it shall be given you; seek, and ye shall find; knock, and it shall be opened unto you: for every one that asketh receiveth; and he that seeketh findeth; and to him that knocked it shall be opened.*

Peace I leave with you, my peace I give unto you: not as the world giveth, give I unto you. Let not your heart be troubled, neither let it be afraid.

Fear not, little flock; for it your Father's good pleasure to give you the kingdom." **JESUS**

MATTHEW 7:7-8; JOHN 14:27; LUKE 12:32

Reason 1

GOD WANTS YOUR ATTENTION

𝔙ery few people give God their undivided attention. Our lives may be filled with work, family, pleasure, business, friends, church, or club activities – just the normal, everyday cares that consume our days. Thoughts of God are often crowded to the side.

Then illness strikes. Work ceases. Family and friends go on with their daily activities without us. Even church work stops. And now, there is finally time to focus on God.

If the sickness is terminal, questions come unbidden about death, God, eternity, and the Bible. God has our attention at last, perhaps for the first time in years. Read about the following men, from the pages of the Bible. God wanted their undivided attention.

It is exciting to read how He got it!

"For I reckon that the sufferings of this present time are not worthy to be compared with the glory which shall be revealed _**in us**_." (Romans 8:18)

A Man Called Saul

Saul was a young man of robust health, with a vitality that equaled his religious fervor. He went from village to town to city, searching for followers of Jesus Christ. He was a self-appointed **Christian Exterminator**.

His appointment was not conceived in the minds of his superiors. He hated Jesus and His disciples so intensely, that he went to the High Priest to receive permission to seize Christians and drag them to Jerusalem to be tried.

He travelled many dusty roads, but he drove himself willingly, because he was a man with one mission: to rid the country of the Jesus followers.

He was almost to Damascus, when he had an experience that would multiply, rather than destroy, Christians!

"And as he journeyed, he came near Damascus: and suddenly there shined round about him a light from heaven: and he fell to the earth, and heard a voice saying unto him, Saul, Saul, why persecutest thou me?

"And he said, Who art thou, Lord? And the Lord said, I am Jesus whom thou persecutest: it is hard for thee to kick against the pricks.

"And he trembling and astonished said, Lord, what wilt thou have me to do? And the Lord said unto him, Arise, and go into the city, and it shall be told thee what thou must do. And the men which journeyed with him stood speechless, hearing a voice, but seeing no man.

"And Saul arose from the earth; and when his eyes were opened, he saw no man: but they led him by the hand, and brought him into Damascus. And he was three days without sight..." (Acts 9:3-9)

Saul began his journey to Damascus with his head held high, his eyes gleaming with hatred, leading his troop of men. Acts 9:1 describes Saul as a man ". . . breathing out threatenings and slaughter against the disciples of the Lord."

When he entered a town, terror would have been in the heart of every Christian. Mothers wondered if Saul would learn that they had committed their lives to the gentle Nazarene called Jesus. If he did, they knew that he would soon be beating on their doors to arrest them, and drag them bound, to Jerusalem.

Would children arrive home to find their parents gone? Or would parents wait in vain for their sons or daughters to arrive home, only to learn later that they had been captured by Saul?

Saul was to the Christians what Hitler would later be to the Jews, and what the Russian KGB became to the followers of Jesus Christ.

The Christians of Damascus waited fearfully for the arrival of the dreaded Saul.

His party entered Damascus. But who was this man, clutching the men beside him and stumbling over pebbles? Could it be Saul, who was being led by the hand as a child?

Nothing could have made Saul as helpless as sudden blindness. A proud, mighty man, who had all the answers and had dared to fight against the Son of God, had been reduced to a staggering, blind man.

"Who art thou, Lord?", this man asked from a voice grown small.

A voice rang from the heavens: "I am Jesus whom thou persecutest."

"**I am JESUS**"...the same Jesus who had walked these roads earlier, touching blind eyes and freely giving the gift of sight.

"**I am JESUS**" ... the same Jesus who had stood in the synagogue and cried, "The Spirit of the Lord is upon me, because he hath anointed me to ...(give) recovering of sight to the blind." (Luke 4:18)

"**I am JESUS**" ... the same Jesus who had walked from city to city, leaving in His path men, women and children praising God, as they stared wide-eyed upon their loved ones, flowers, trees, the sun, grass, and colors, for the very first time.

This same Jesus had now appeared to a seeing man, called Saul, and left him blind.

Saul came face to face with this Jesus, and he looked up to the heavens with one burning question: "Who art thou, Lord?"

Jesus looked upon Saul, and He saw a man fighting and blaspheming Him with every ounce of his energy.

And Jesus loved him.

The same love that reached out and touched the blind and made them see, now reached out to Saul, touched his seeing eyes, and made them blind.

As a result of his head-on encounter with Jesus Christ, Paul turned from a raging enemy of God to a loving son of God.

Could it be that God has touched you, and made you sick, so you would humble yourself and ask, "Who art thou, Lord? What wilt thou have me to do?"

A King Called Nebuchadnezzar

Pride. It rears itself up in many forms: in a man who looks down from his pedestal upon the rest of humanity;

as a man looking eye to eye at God, rather than falling upon his face before Him; or by a man crediting himself for his accomplishments, rather than giving thanks to God for his blessings.

Whatever the form, God calls all pride an abomination. If anyone had cause to be proud, it was Nebuchadnezzar - the King of Babylon. For Babylon was the city that ruled the world. That made King Nebuchadnezzar the ruler of the world. His word could command armies to march and conquer. One of his fingers could condemn anyone in the world to death. He could have everything he wanted, when he wanted it.

He was strutting through his palace one day, viewing his priceless treasures. Can you hear him boasting: "Is not this great Babylon, that I have built for the house of the kingdom by the might of **my power** and for the honour of **my majesty**?" (Daniel 4:30)

His proud words reached the ears of a greater King than Nebuchadnezzar. God, the Creator of all the lands Nebuchadnezzar thought he ruled, and the One who gave Nebuchadnezzar life, was moved to humble this king.

Nebuchadnezzar was about to meet One who was far more powerful than he was.

"While the word was in the king's mouth, there fell a voice from heaven, saying, O king Nebuchadnezzar, to thee it is spoken; The kingdom is departed from thee. And they shall drive thee from men, and thy dwelling shall be with the beasts of the field: they shall make thee to eat grass as oxen, and seven times shall pass over thee, **until thou know that the most High ruleth in the kingdom of men**, and giveth it to whomsoever he will.

"The same hour was the thing fulfilled upon Nebuchadnezzar: and he was driven from men, and did eat grass as oxen, and his body was wet with the dew of heaven, till his hairs were grown like eagles' feathers, and his nails like birds' claws."

Here, in King Nebuchadnezzar's own words, is what happened next.

"And at the end of the days I Nebuchadnezzar lifted up mine eyes unto heaven, and mine understanding returned unto me, and **I blessed the most High**, and **I praised and honoured him that liveth for ever**, whose dominion is an everlasting dominion, and **his kingdom** is from generation to generation: and all the inhabitants of the earth are reputed as nothing: and **he doeth according to his will in the army of heaven**, and among the inhabitants of the earth: and none can stay his hand, or say unto him, What doest thou?

"At the same time my reason returned unto me; and for the glory of my kingdom, mine honour and brightness returned unto me; and my counsellors and my lords sought unto me; and I was established in my kingdom, and excellent majesty was added unto me.

"**Now** I Nebuchadnezzar **praise and extol and honour** the **King of heaven**, all whose works are truth, and his ways judgment: and **those that walk in pride he is able to abase**." (Daniel 4:31-37)

King Nebuchadnezzar was struck with mental illness! This powerful king was instantly reduced to a man without reason and understanding. He was rejected by men and driven from men.

He no longer proudly reigned in his palace, but lived with the animals of the field. His menu became grass.

Children were frightened, as they looked upon this half-man, half-animal, covered with hair, with claws extending from his fingers.

With one touch, God had shown King Nebuchadnezzar three things:

1. **God was, and is, in control.**
2. **God is the Source of all blessings.**
3. **Without God, man is nothing**.

Those days of insanity were terrible days.

Nebuchadnezzar, who believed he was in control of his kingdom, learned that **he was not even in control of his own mind**!

But his days of mental illness proved to be more profitable to the king than all of the days he had lived in wealth, power, and splendor.

For his sickness caused him to turn to God.

Before his sanity left him, King Nebuchadnezzar bragged about ***his*** accomplishments, ***his*** power, ***his*** honor, and ***his*** majesty.

When his sanity returned, King Nebuchadnezzar said: "Now I Nebuchadnezzar praise and extol and honour the King of heaven, all whose works are truth!"

One thing caused this great king to acknowledge God – **his sickness**.

God loved King Nebuchadnezzar, but hated the pride that stood between them. What better way to destroy his pride, than to touch his brain with a sickness that caused him to become more animal than human?

For the first time in his life, King Nebuchadnezzar was moved to acknowledge God as **GOD**!

Don't rebel when you are sick! Turn your sickness into the greatest blessing of your life!

"Humble yourself in the sight of the Lord, and he shall lift you up!" (James 4:10)

Repent to God. Confess your sins, your pride, and your stubborn and rebellious ways. Receive Jesus Christ as your personal Savior. Ask God to cleanse you from all of your sins with the blood that poured from Jesus' broken body on the cross of Calvary. Ask Jesus to come live a new life ***in you*** and ***through you!*** Then you can say, as King Nebuchadnezzar said after his sickness: "**NOW** I praise and extol and honour the **KING** of heaven!"

A Captain Called Naaman

Naaman. The Bible says of him: "Now Naaman, captain of the host of the king of Syria, was a great man with his master, and honourable ... a mighty man in valour."

Then five fateful words are added to his description: "... **but he was a leper**." (II Kings 5:1)

Leprosy is a disease with such terrible dread attached to its name, that it has recently been renamed "Hansen's disease".

In earlier times, it was a sickness that caused its

8

bearers to be banished from family and friends and cry "Unclean! Unclean!" when approached.

Even today, with all of our medical advances, no cure for leprosy has been found. We can then imagine the joy and fearful anticipation Naaman had, when he heard about a prophet in Israel who could cure people of leprosy.

Naaman was desperate to be healed. He travelled in his chariot to Israel, taking with him a letter from his king and ten talents of silver, six-thousand pieces of gold, and ten changes of raiment to pay for his cure.

After a disappointing visit with Israel's king, Naaman finally arrived at Elisha's house.

Elisha sent his servant to the door with a message for Naaman. Naaman listened to the message with shock and horror. "Go and wash in Jordan seven times, and thy flesh shall come again to thee, and thou shalt be clean." (II Kings 5:10)

Naaman whirled away from the door, fuming with anger. He had travelled all the way from Syria, and Elisha had not even bothered to answer the door or invite him into his house. Instead, he delivered his message through a mere servant, and sent him on his way. And what a message! He was to go wash in the filthy Jordan River seven times - as if a dirty river could cure him of leprosy!

Naaman's response revealed his wrath. "I thought, He will surely come out to me, and stand, and call on the name of the Lord **his** God, and strike his hand over the place, and recover the leper. Are not Abana and Pharpar, rivers of Damascus, better than all the waters of Israel? may I not wash in them, and be clean? So he turned and went away in a rage."

Naaman's servant then said to him: "My father, if the prophet had bid thee do some great thing, wouldest thou not have done it? how much rather then, when he saith to thee, Wash, and be clean?

"Then went he down, and dipped himself seven times in Jordan, according to the saying of the man of God: and his flesh came again like unto the flesh of a little child, and he was clean. And he returned to the man of God, he and all his company, and came, and stood before him: and he said, Behold, **now I know that there is no God in all the earth, but in Israel**."

When Elisha refused to take gifts from Naaman (unlike many "ministers" today who promise healing if a donation is given), Naaman made this vow to Elisha: "Thy servant will henceforth offer neither burnt offering nor sacrifice unto other gods, but unto *the Lord*." (II Kings 5:11-17.)

Naaman no longer referred to God as Elisha's God. He called Him the Lord!

Listen again to his words.

"Now I know … God!"

"Henceforth (I will) offer …unto the Lord."

If Naaman had not been a leper, he would have had no reason to seek healing, and he would not have found God!

Naaman's leprosy was a blessing that led him to God!

Is your sickness a blessing? It can be, if it causes you to turn to God and find salvation for your soul!

You will spend your eternity in perfect health, praising

God for loving you enough to bring you to Him through a sickness that resulted in your salvation!

Don't make the mistake Naaman nearly made. His pride almost kept him from being healed and serving God!

Naaman's only opportunity for healing was to bathe in the Jordan River. He did not want to do it. He had imagined on his way to Israel how he would be healed, and he did not expect to have to humble himself.

Perhaps you have already planned how you are going to come to God for salvation. Your thoughts may have placed you in a fine church, or in a private audience with a preacher or a priest. But if you truly want spiritual healing, there is only one order, and it comes through God's servants, as they deliver His message: **"Go wash in the blood of Jesus, and be clean!"**

Is your pride keeping you from being cleansed by the blood Jesus shed? Remember the words of Naaman's servants: "If the prophet had bid thee do some great thing, wouldest thou not have done it? How much rather then, when he saith to thee, **Wash, and be clean**?"

Naaman was prepared to pay for his healing with gold and silver. But *Elisha refused the payment*. You may be willing to do a great thing for God and may even offer Him money, but He says: "You were not redeemed with corruptible things, as silver and gold ... but with the precious blood of Christ." (I Peter 1:18-19)

God may have given you a sickness so you will listen to His invitation:

"Come now, and let us reason together, saith the Lord:

though your sins be as scarlet, they shall be as white as snow; though they be red like crimson, they shall be as wool. The blood of Jesus Christ His Son, cleanseth us from all sin. If we confess our sins, he is faithful and just to forgive us our sins, and to cleanse us from all unrighteousness." (Isaiah 1:18 and I John 1:7 & 9)

God has made salvation so simple. Yet, many refuse to humble themselves and wash in the blood Jesus shed on Calvary's cross. Instead, they offer money, service, good works, or some great thing – and go from God's presence, unwashed, filthy, still in need of healing for their souls.

It was wonderful that Naaman was healed of leprosy. It would be wonderful if you would be healed of your sickness. However, sin cannot even be compared to the physical diseases of leprosy or cancer. Sin is fatal – and its result is eternal death.

Romans 6:23 tells us: "For the wages of sin is death."

If God is calling you through your sickness, go to Him, be cleansed of your sins, and your sickness will become your greatest blessing. Like Naaman, it will lead you straight to God, and you will find the wonderful salvation He has for you.

Conclusion

God may have allowed you to be sick, so He can draw you to His Son, Jesus, to be saved.

God is more concerned about your soul than your body. Your soul will experience eternal life or eternal death. If it takes a sickness to your mortal body to bring healing to your eternal soul, He will use it! He has done it in the past to Saul, Nebuchadnezzar, and Naaman — and our changeless God will do it today. He will do this, because He loves you and values your soul, even more than He valued the body of His only begotten, beloved Son. He sent Him to earth to save your soul.

Read the following messages, taken from the pages of the Bible:

JESUS: "And if thy hand offend thee, cut it off: it is better for thee to enter into life **maimed**, than having two hands to go into hell, into the fire that never shall be quenched: where their worm dieth not, and the fire is not quenched ... and if thy foot offend thee, cut it off: it is better for thee to enter **halt** into life, than having two feet to be cast into hell, into the fire that never shall be quenched: where their worm dieth not, and the fire is not quenched ... and if thine eye offend thee, pluck it out: it is better for thee to enter into the kingdom of God with **one eye**, than having two eyes to be cast into hell fire: where their worm dieth not, and the fire is not quenched. For what is a man profited, if he shall gain the whole world, and lose his own soul? or what shall a man give in exchange for his soul?" (Mark 9:43-48 and Matthew 16:26)

JOB: "Our days upon earth are a shadow." (Job 8:9)

DAVID: "It is good for me that I have been afflicted; that I might learn thy statutes." (Psalm 119:71)

JAMES: "For what is your life? It is even a vapour, that appeareth for a little time, and then vanisheth away." (James 4:14)

JOHN: "And I saw a new heaven and a new earth ... and God shall wipe away all tears from their eyes; and there shall be no more death, neither sorrow, nor crying, neither shall there be *any more pain*: for the former things are passed away." (Revelation 21:1 & 4)

How can we even compare our souls, that will live either in heaven or hell forever, to our bodies that will live on this earth for probably less than 100 years?

The Bible calls our lives in the body a mere shadow; a vapor.

Jesus tells us that it is far better to spend our lives on earth maimed, halt, crippled, without an eye, or without a hand, than to spend an eternity in the fires of hell.

If you want God to save you, and can pray the following prayer from a sincere heart, do it right now.

"God, I come to you in the name of Jesus. Forgive me for my sins. Wash me in the blood that Jesus shed for me. Come into my heart and take control of my life. Change me. Make me your child. I believe that Jesus is Your only begotten Son. I receive Him, as my personal Savior, and the Lord of my life."

After praying this prayer, talk to God in your own words. Confess your specific sins to Him, and ask Him to forgive you. Thank Him for sending Jesus to die in your place. Tell Him your honest feelings. Ask Him to give you power to live the rest of your life for Him. Thank Him for His love. *And thank Him for your sickness that drew you to Him for spiritual healing.*

The Psalmist said, "*Before* I was afflicted I went astray: but *now* have I kept thy word." (Psalm 119:67)

I want to tell you about a man named Joe. His family and friends gathered from far and wide to celebrate his eightieth birthday. But not one of them could lift Joe's spirit. When Joe was asked about his life, he said: "You all believe I had a wonderful life. Yes, I had wonderful parents. Yes, I've been wealthy. Yes, I married a beautiful wife who loves me, as I love her. I have good children, and have been blessed with good health. But let me tell you why I am unhappy today.

"I cannot quit thinking about just one certain day of my eighty years. I was 41 years old. I overslept, and I was late to work. The parking places were already full, making me even later. I had to walk two blocks in the rain. My umbrella was not in the car, and I was drenched. My boss was angry. One of my co-workers refused to answer my greeting. Then I received a telephone call from my wife. My daughter had hit a tree while parking, and her brand new car was dented. I was afraid my co-worker would snub me again, so I skipped lunch. I couldn't take two rebuffs in one day. When I finally finished my long day at work, I went home, ready for a good meal. Dinner was not ready. By that time, I had a terrible headache. I was ready to give up. I went to bed hungry. Now you know why I am having trouble celebrating what you call my good life. That one terrible day in my past ruins this day for me."

By now, you must realize that Joe is a figment of my imagination.

But can you imagine entering into the splendors of heaven for eternity – and thinking about your "one bad day" on earth?

The Bible does not refer to our earthly lives as a day, but as *a vapor; a smoke; and a passing shadow*. (James 4:14; Psalm 102:3; I Chronicles 29:15; and Psalm 144:4).

How can what we call a hard life on earth be compared to an eternity of splendor in heaven? God has promised us perfect health - an incorruptible and immortal body – forever!

No matter what we go through in this life, it will be as nothing in the endless light of eternity!

All of life's trials, that have drawn us to Jesus, will be worth it all, when we see Him, and begin our first ten million years in heaven!

Here is Paul's description of his life on earth.

He said he was "in labours more abundant, in stripes above measure, in prisons more frequent, in deaths oft. Of the Jews five times received I forty stripes save one. Thrice was I beaten with rods, once was I stoned, thrice I suffered shipwreck, a night and a day I have been in the deep; in journeyings often, in perils of waters, in perils of robbers, in perils by mine own countrymen, in perils by the heathen, in perils in the city, in perils in the wilderness, in perils in the sea, in perils among false brethren; in weariness and painfulness, in watchings often, in hunger and thirst, in fastings often, in cold and nakedness." (II Corinthians 11:23-27)

And this is how Paul summed up his hard life: "For I reckon that the sufferings of this present time are not worthy to be compared with the glory which shall be revealed in us." (Romans 8:18)

Compared to Paul's life (or most anyone's), Joe had absolutely nothing to complain about. Yet, there are so many Joes today, who complain when the least thing goes wrong.

Perhaps your life has been far different than Joe's.

You may have suffered with a debilitating sickness your entire life. Perhaps you have spent years bedridden, or bound to a wheel chair.

Begin to think of your life here as a vapor – a smoke – a breath – just a passing shadow.

Colossians 3:1-4 counsels us: "If ye then be risen with Christ, seek those things which are above, where Christ sitteth on the right hand of God. *Set your affection on things above, not on things on the earth.* For ye are dead, and your life is hid with Christ in God. When Christ, **who is our life**, shall appear, then shall *ye also appear with him in glory.*"

Isaiah 65:17 is a beautiful promise: "For, behold, I create new heavens and a new earth: and *the former shall not be remembered, nor come into mind*."

If you have never received Jesus in your life as your Savior; you do not want Him to be part of your life; and if you refuse to ask Him to save you, you may as well put this book down. It has no answers for one who is rebellious toward God.

Elisha had only one message for Naaman. If Naaman had continued to rebel against God's message, he would have returned to Syria with his leprosy.

If you have turned to God, in humility and repentance for salvation, there is further help for you in the following pages.

If you were already a child of God when you began reading this book, study the following reasons to your question, *"**God, why am I sick?**"*, to find your personal answer.

Reason 2 may cause you to wonder if you will pass or fail God's test – **TO PROVE US**!

Reason 2

TO PROVE US

God uses many things to prove (test) His people. He led Moses and the Israelites in the wilderness for forty years.

When the forty years were finished, Moses told the people: "Thou shalt remember all the way which the Lord thy God led thee these forty years in the wilderness, **to humble thee**, and **to prove thee, to know what was in thine heart, whether thou wouldest keep his commandments, or no**." (Deuteronomy 8:2)

Many proved to be unfaithful during their time of testing. Only a few passed their tests, and remained faithful to God.

Genesis 22:1 says that "God did **tempt** (**prove**) Abraham."

God commanded Abraham to sacrifice his son, Isaac.

Abraham prepared himself and the altar in obedience to God. It took a voice crying from heaven to stop Abraham at the last moment.

"Lay not thine hand upon the lad, neither do thou any thing unto him: for **now I know** that thou fearest God, seeing thou hast not withheld thy son, thine only son from me." (Genesis 22:12)

God proved the Israelites to see if they would remain faithful to Him, even when their journey was hard. And God proved Abraham to see if his love for God would surpass his love for his son.

God also proved Job. One of the things He used to test Job's trust was sickness.

Satan came before God, and God challenged him with these words: "Hast thou considered my servant Job, that there is none like him in the earth, a perfect and an upright man, one that feareth God and escheweth (shuns) evil?"

Satan answered with a challenge of his own. "Doth Job fear God for nought? Hast not thou made an hedge about him, and about his house, and about all that he hath on every side? Thou hast blessed the work of his hands, and his substance is increased in the land. But ***put forth thine hand now, and touch all that he hath, and he will curse thee to thy face***." (Job 1:8-11)

God took His hedge down as a result of that challenge, and Satan moved in to destroy Job. In one day, Job lost 7,000 sheep, 3,000 camels, 500 yoke of oxen, 500 she asses, his servants, his seven sons, and his three daughters. ***Job's testing time had begun***.

His response to all of these overwhelming tragedies is almost as unbelievable to us today, as it probably was to Satan, as he waited anxiously for Job to curse God. He was no doubt sure that Job's words of rebellion would erupt angrily from his crushed heart.

"Then Job arose, and rent his mantle, and shaved his head, and fell down upon the ground, and ***worshipped***, and said, Naked came I out of my mother's womb, and naked shall I return thither: the Lord gave, and the Lord hath taken away; ***blessed be the name of the Lord***.

"In all this, Job sinned not, nor charged God foolishly." (Job 1:20-22)

Most of us know someone who has rebelled and turned against God because of the death of one child. Job lost all ten of his children in one day – and fell before God to worship Him.

The next time Satan appeared before God, God asked him, "Hast thou considered my servant Job, that there is none like him in the earth, a perfect and an upright man, one that feareth God, and escheweth evil? And still he holdeth fast his integrity, although thou movedst me against him, to destroy him without cause."

Satan answered with another challenge. "... put forth thine hand now, and touch **his bone** and **his flesh**, and *he will curse thee to thy face*. And the Lord said unto Satan, Behold, he is in thine hand; but save his life. So went Satan forth from the presence of the Lord, and smote Job with sore boils from the sole of his foot unto his crown." (Job 2:3 & 5-7)

Job had passed one test. He remained faithful to God, even though he lost his possessions, his servants, and his children.

But now came the second test.

Job's body was viciously attacked. His health failed.

He sat among ashes and scraped himself with a potsherd (piece of broken crockery). His mourning wife, who had shared his devastating losses, stood looking down at her pitiful husband. Her advice to him was: "Curse God and die."

Job looked up at her and said: "Thou speaketh as one of the foolish women speaketh. What? Shall we receive good at the hand of God, and shall we not receive evil? In all this did not Job sin with his lips."

His health did not return. Sickness raged in his broken body, and he was an outcast. Listen to his moans: "Wearisome nights are appointed to me. I am full of tossings to and fro unto the dawning of the day. My flesh is clothed with worms and clods of dust; my skin is broken, and become loathsome. My face is foul with weeping, and on my eyelids is the shadow of death. My days are … spent without hope." (Job 2:9-10; 7:3-5; 16:16; 7:6)

He became despondent. Depression settled within his heart.

"I should have been as though I had not been; I should have been carried from the womb to the grave." (Job 10:19)

His faith in a loving God began to waver. He looked up to the heavens, and cried, "Wherefore hidest thou thy face, and holdest me for thine enemy?" (Job 13:24)

Job went through a time of rebellion. As the days wore on without change, his hope faded.

During the first days of his sickness, he had said of God, "(He) doeth great things past finding out; yea, and wonders without number. Who will say unto him, What doest thou? How much less shall I answer him, and choose out my words to reason with him?" (Job 9:10 & 12 and Job 9:12 & 14)

He got sicker. In his despair, he cried out to God, "See thou mine affliction; for it increaseth!"

He confessed, "I am full of confusion! I will speak in the bitterness of my soul." (Job 10:15-16 & 1)

He longed to appear before God with his questions. "Oh that I knew where I might find him! that I might come even to his seat! I would order my cause before him, and fill my mouth with arguments." (Job 23:3-4)

Then trust in his God began to again stir in Job's heart, driving his confusion away. *"Though he slay me, yet will I trust in him*!" (Job 13:15)

Faith again filled his soul, and he declared from his tormented, diseased body: "I know that my redeemer liveth, and that he shall stand at the latter day upon this earth: and though after my skin worms destroy this body, yet in my flesh shall I see God! Whom I shall see for myself, and mine eyes shall behold, and not another." (Job 19:25-27)

Job proved to be faithful. He passed his test!

Satan stood defeated before God. He had tried his best to destroy Job's faith in God and his love for God.

He failed.

Job's faith remained steadfast and unmovable.

When the testing time was completed, God touched Job again with His hand of blessing. "So the Lord blessed the latter end of Job more than his beginning!" (Job 42:12)

He gave him 14,000 sheep; 6,000 camels, 1,000 yoke of oxen, and 1,000 she asses; seven sons, three beautiful daughters, and 140 more years of abundant life!

James 5:11 says: "Behold, we count them happy which endure. Ye have heard of the *patience of Job*, and have seen the end of the Lord; that the Lord is very pitiful, and of tender mercy."

A proving time...

Man invents things for our use upon earth, and we fully expect these inventions to be tested and proven before they are sold. They are put through conditions of extreme stress and strain and tested for their endurance.

Should we then think it strange that God has a proving time? He tests us to see if we will endure stress and strain – and yes, *even sickness* – and remain strong and faithful to Him.

The Apostle Peter's advice still rings out to us, down through the ages: "Beloved, think it not strange concerning the fiery trial which is to try you, as though some strange thing happened unto you: but rejoice, inasmuch as ye are partakers of Christ's *sufferings*; that, when his glory shall be revealed, ye may be glad also with exceeding joy." (I Peter 4:12-13)

Job said, "When he hath **tried me**, I shall come forth as gold." (Job 23:10)

He was right. When his trial was nearly over, he said to God, "I have heard of thee by the hearing of the ear: but *now* mine eye seeth thee. Wherefore I abhor myself, and repent in dust and ashes." (Job 42:5-6)

After his trial, he was closer to God than he had ever been.

God desires this close relationship with all of us. Revelation 4:11 teaches us that we are created for *God's pleasure*.

John tells us that "...our *fellowship* is with the Father, and with his Son Jesus Christ." (I John 1:3)

He has called us to be His sons, His daughters, and the bride of His only begotten Son. (II Corinthians 6:18 and 11:2)

Peter said: "Wherein ye greatly rejoice, though now

for a season, if need be, ye are in heaviness through manifold temptations: that the ***trial of your faith,*** being much more precious than of gold that perisheth, though it be ***tried with fire***, might be found unto praise and honour and glory at the appearing of Jesus Christ." (I Peter 1:6-7)

Our faith in God is far more valuable than all the gold in the world.

I John 5:4 says that "...this is the victory that over-cometh the world, even **our faith**."

We read that He will "... present you holy and unblameable and unreproveable in his sight ... **if ye continue in the faith** grounded and settled." (Colossians 1:22-23)

The apostle Paul kept his faith. He described part of his trials: "Five times received I forty stripes save one. Thrice was I beaten with rods, once was I stoned, thrice I suffered shipwreck, a night and a day I have been in the deep; in journeyings often, in perils of waters, in perils of robbers, in perils by mine own countrymen, in perils by the heathen, in perils in the city, in perils in the wilderness, in perils in the sea, in perils among false brethren; in weariness and ***painfulness***, in watchings often, in hunger and thirst, in fastings often, in cold and nakedness." (II Corinthians 11:24-27)

Paul concluded his report with this startling statement, "I take pleasure in **infirmities (*medical conditions that cause physical weakness; illnesses*)**, in reproaches, in necessities, in persecutions, in distresses for Christ's sake!" (II Corinthians 12:10)

Paul didn't just endure – he took pleasure in his trials!

He said that he was persuaded "... that neither death, nor life, nor angels, nor principalities, nor powers, nor things present, nor things to come, nor height, nor depth, nor any other creature, shall be able to separate us from the love of God, which is in Christ Jesus our Lord." (Romans 8:38-39)

The prophet, Habakkuk, had this same unshakeable faith.

He wrote: "Although the fig tree shall not blossom, neither shall fruit be in the vines; the labour of the olive shall fail, and the fields shall yield no meat; the flock shall be cut off from the fold, and there shall be no herd in the stalls: yet I will rejoice in the God of my salvation." (Habakkuk 3:17-18)

Does our faith in God endure only when everything is going good for us? If all our prayers were instantly answered – why would God refer to **trials** of our **faith**? We would have nothing to endure!

The unwavering faith of men of old during trials and even martyrdom is recorded for us, in Hebrews 11:36-38: "They "had **trials** of cruel mockings and scourgings, yea, moreover of bonds and imprisonment: they were stoned, they were sawn asunder, were tempted, were slain with the sword: they wandered about in sheepskins and goatskins; being destitute, **afflicted**, **tormented**... they wandered in deserts, and in mountains, and in dens and caves of the earth."

Does our faith compare to theirs? Could we be faithful to Christ, even if it meant giving our lives?

Or are we unable to even endure a sickness, without turning our backs on God?

Jesus was concerned about finding followers with faith at the time of His second coming.

Listen to His words: "When the Son of man cometh, shall he **find faith** on the earth?" (Luke 18:8)

No wonder He gives us trials! He wants to strengthen **our faith!** He does this, because He loves us! According to His Word, our faith is far more valuable than gold! We would all rejoice if we found gold on our land. Yet, when God gives us trials to increase and strengthen our faith, we rebel and question His love for us.

Conclusion

God may be proving your faith in Him, through a sickness, as He did with Job.

Stand fast!

God's Word has one consistent message, from Genesis to Revelation!

God loves you. If you doubt His love – look at the cross!

Trust Him!

Make up your mind to keep your faith in Him and trust His love for you – in sickness and in health!

Wedding vows often include promises to remain faithful to one's husband or wife "for richer or poorer; for better or worse; *in sickness and in health*."

When we become the bride of Christ, we also need to pledge our faithful love to Him – for richer or poorer; for better or worse – and *in sickness and in health.*

Job kept his faith in God through his severe trial. He

came through his tragic days with a closer relationship with God and more abundant blessings.

Job lived the Psalmist's words: "Many are the afflictions of the righteous: but the Lord delivereth him out of them all." (Psalm 34:19)

He discovered that "weeping may endure for a night, but joy cometh in the morning." (Psalm 30:5)

Let God work in His way in your life!

Endure the trial!

Pass the test!

"But the God of all grace, who hath called us unto his eternal glory by Christ Jesus, after that ye have *suffered* a while, make you perfect, stablish, strengthen, settle you. To him be glory and dominion for ever and ever. Amen." (I Peter 5:10-11)

Examine Yourself

Is your sickness a **test** of your faith?

Is God **proving** your love for Him?

Have you made a decision to keep loving God – in *sickness* and in health?

If you have previously made only a half-hearted commitment to God, this may be the reason you are sick.

God may have allowed your sickness, so you would examine your dedication to Him.

Now is the time to make a whole-hearted commitment to love and serve God and to trust His love for you.

If you have already been trusting God completely, and your faith in Him has not wavered even during your sickness – read on!

There are five more reasons why people are sick. One of them could be your answer!

In fact – it could be that you are sick because God is calling you ... **TO MINISTER!**

Reason 3

TO MINISTER

"**I** was sick," Jesus told His faithful followers, "and ye visited me."

"When saw we thee sick?" the righteous ones asked Jesus in amazement.

Can you see His smile, as Jesus answered them: "Inasmuch as ye have done it unto one of the least of these my brethren, ye have done it unto me."

Then His smile faded, as He turned to the group on His left hand, and His words became sharp: "I was ... sick, and ye visited me not!"

They probably stared at Him in astonishment, as they asked, "When saw we thee sick?"

"Inasmuch as ye did it not to one of the least of these, ye did it not to me," their Judge said sternly. Then He pronounced the verdict that would seal their fate. "These shall go away into everlasting punishment." (Matthew 25:36-37, 40, 43-45)

God expects His servants to follow the example Jesus left for us. Jesus spent much of His time on earth ministering to the sick. He walked miles of dusty roads to minister healing to people with fevers, palsy, leprosy, and other diseases.

Today, we are His body. I Corinthians 12:27 clearly teaches us: "Now **ye** are the body of Christ."

We are His feet that should be walking the roads in

search of the sick. We are His hands that should be comforting and ministering His healing touch. We are His lips that should speak His name and of God's love. We are His ears that should forever listen for the cries of hurting people. We are His eyes that should be looking upon others with tender mercy. We are His heart that should ache with a compassion that compels our bodies to minister God's love – even when we are weary with service.

Are we faithful to such a high calling?

Jesus said, "He that believeth on me, **the works that I do shall he do also**." (John 14:12)

Follow Jesus' steps for just one day of His sojourn on earth. Feel His joy, His hurt, His weariness.

He was eating on this day with His disciples, when many publicans and sinners came and interrupted His dinner.

The Pharisees were present also, and as always, they were criticizing Him. Jesus was speaking to them, when John's disciples came along, questioning Him because His disciples were eating, rather than fasting.

While Jesus was answering them, a man hurried through the door, crying, "My daughter is dead!"

Jesus and His disciples left their meal, and began their walk to the ruler's house.

While on their way, a woman, who was desperate for His healing power, reached out and touched the hem of Jesus' garment. He paused to speak healing words to her, then went on.

He arrived at the ruler's house and made His way through mourners. Their wails turned to scornful jeers, when He claimed the girl was not dead, but only asleep.

He reached out and lifted the ruler's daughter from death's door, and left the house with its shocked mourners and rejoicing parents.

Two blind men followed Him back to the house, pleading for His attention and mercy. He opened their eyes. As they ran out to look upon the world, a dumb man, possessed with a devil, was dragged to Him. Jesus set the captive man free, and his tongue was loosed to praise God.

"He casteth out devils through the prince of the devils," the Pharisees sneered.

This was just **one day** with Jesus. It is recorded in Matthew 9:10-34. It is little wonder that John said, after writing about the life of Jesus, "And there are also many other things which Jesus did, the which, if they should be written every one, I suppose that even the world itself could not contain the books that should be written!" (John 21:25)

Jesus is our example. God expects us to walk in His steps. "For even hereunto were ye called: because Christ also suffered for us, leaving us an example, that **ye should follow his steps**." (I Peter 2:21)

Jesus gave Himself unreservedly to minister to people with needs. "And Jesus went about all the cities and villages, teaching in their synagogues, and preaching the gospel of the kingdom, and **healing every sickness and every disease** among the people. But when He saw the multitudes, he was moved with **compassion** on them." (Matthew 9:35-36)

As a member of the body of Christ, are you moved

with compassion?

Compassion literally moved Jesus from city to village.

Compassion kept His tired feet walking.

Compassion moved His aching arm to reach out and lay His hand on one more sick person.

Perhaps you are a member of Christ's body who is unmoved when you hear of another's need. You may be one who hears of a sick person and prays a hurried prayer: "God bless my sister. Heal her, Lord! Comfort her! Amen!"

Amen. It is done. Your responsibility to her is done. Your concern for her is done. Your prayer is done.

Jesus did not say, "I was sick and you **prayed** for me not." He said, "I was sick, and ye **visited** me not!"

He said, "These signs shall follow them that believe... in my name...they shall **lay hands** on the **sick**, and they shall recover." (Mark 16:17-18)

You cannot lay hands on someone from a distance. You need to go to the sick to minister to them.

You need to visit them.

"God, why am I sick?"

Could it be God has put you in a hospital, because it is the only way to get you there to **visit the sick**?

Most people accept Christ as their Savior during a time of crisis. There are multitudes of sick people who could find Christ during their sicknesses, and be healed from the deadliest disease of all - **sin**. But where are the Christians who minister the Word of life in the hospitals and nursing homes? Are you one who has left all the ministry to your pastor or a chaplain, while you seek pleasure, money, or relaxation in front of your television set or on the golf course?

Jesus did not say, "These signs shall follow **pastors**." He said the signs shall follow **believers**!

Your responsibility to your neighbor or relative is not finished when you pray a prayer and ask your pastor to call on him. Your responsibility is to be a personal witness and a comfort to him.

II Corinthians 1:3-4 says: "Blessed be God, even the Father of our Lord Jesus Christ, the Father of mercies, and the God of all comfort; who comforteth us in all our tribulation, that *we may be able to comfort them* which are in *any trouble,* by the comfort wherewith we ourselves are comforted of God."

Would the jailor of Philippi have been saved, if Paul and Silas had not been arrested and placed in his custody? They had committed no crime, but were imprisoned for teaching and preaching Christ.

"We won't have it!" the magistrates of the city cried. Paul and Silas were severely beaten and thrust into the dungeon in stocks. The prisoners awoke at midnight to a sound they had undoubtedly never heard in the prison. Paul and Silas were singing!

And can you imagine the shock of the jailor? He heard his two newest prisoners joyfully praising the Lord, their songs echoing through the walls of the prison.

Suddenly, the prison floors and walls began to shake. Locked doors were flung open with a crash. Chains, that had secured prisoners, fell from their bodies. The jailor, who was held responsible for the security of the prison, prepared to kill himself. He knew that he would face certain death by the hand of his superiors, because he had failed to secure the prison.

But a voice shouted from the inner cell: "Do thyself no harm! We are all here!"

The night ended with the jailor and his entire family being saved and baptized! (Verses from Acts 16: 22-34)

Would that family be in heaven today, if Paul and Silas had not been beaten and imprisoned?

Has God put you where you are, to minister to one you would not have met, **had you not been sick?**

Is there someone in your hospital room who needs salvation?

Most of us have heard of Joni Eareckson. She sits bound to a wheelchair, hour after hour, day after day, month after month, year after year.

She begged God to heal her, but she remains paralyzed.

Has God forsaken her? No!

Joni, with her radiant testimony and steadfast faith in her heavenly Father who loves her, has won countless souls to the Lord. She ministers to multitudes of the sick and the helpless. She discovered the God of all comfort in her sickness. Now she comforts others with that same comfort she received.

Would her ministry reach both the sick and the well people, if she was not paralyzed? Would she have a story to tell through her books that have ministered to many thousands?

Joni will be healed – if not in this life, then in the next, where there will be no tears, sorrow, crying, pain, or wheelchairs.

The greatest healing of all is the healing of a sin-sick

soul. That can only be done in this life.

Sometimes ministry can be given more effectively through a weakened body.

"My strength is made perfect in weakness," God told Paul. (II Corinthians 12:9)

Some of the spiritually strongest people are those with a nearly useless body. Christians who have lived for God, in spite of their physical condition, will not only be completely whole in heaven, but they have the additional promise that "they that turn many to righteousness (shall shine) as the stars for ever and ever!" (Daniel 12:3)

God's joy shines more clearly through a person who has little cause to be joyful. His peace is clearly seen through one whose life has been nearly shattered.

A man was often wheeled into our church, when we served in Michigan. He had a beautiful voice that soared above others in the song service, and never failed to bring tears to our eyes.

Lester was blind. But he was not only blind – he had no legs.

But Lester had something many healthy people do not have. He had unceasing joy and a constant testimony that shamed all of us for our complaints. Just listening to him sing praises to God and testify of the Lord's wonders and grace, ministered to all of us who were privileged to hear him.

Would Lester's ministry have been as effective if he had a whole body? Would he have spent time ministering in the nursing home, if that had not been his home? Would he have brought cheer to both residents and staff, if he had not needed to be cared for himself?

God's desire and will for us is to minister to Him, by ministering to others.

He gave us a perfect example of unselfish ministry, through the life of His perfect Son.

Jesus always looked beyond His own needs and saw the needs of others. John 9:1 is an amazing verse: "And *as Jesus passed by*, *he saw* a man which was blind from his birth."

Now read the preceding verse, in John 8:59: "Then took they up stones to cast at him: but Jesus hid himself, and went out of the temple, going through the midst of them, and so passed by. *And as Jesus passed by, he saw*..."

Jesus was being threatened by men who were filled with such raging hatred that they were preparing to stone Him.

Yet Jesus was not looking at them – or even thinking about them. He was not even looking at the stones they held ready to hurl at Him.

He looked beyond His persecutors, and saw a blind man who needed His touch!

Are we so *blinded* by our own needs that we never see the needs of those around us?

Jesus never failed to see one who needed Him!

Now let us look at a later time in Jesus' ministry on earth. He was in one of His favorite places to pray. He lay on His face in the quiet garden, and as His disciples slept nearby, He poured out His heart to His Father.

Suddenly, the sound of marching feet intruded the hallowed spot. The disciples abruptly awoke, and discovered that they were surrounded with a great multitude of angry men, armed with swords and staves.

Peter leaped up and pushed through the incited mob to Jesus. He lifted his sword to protect His Master, and its keen blade sliced off the right ear of Malchus, the high priest's servant.

The dark hour of Christ's mission to earth was about to take place. A menacing mob surrounded Him. One of His own disciples had just betrayed Him with a kiss. His own people, the Jews, had rejected Him. He knew that He was facing an agonizing death at their hands. Yet Jesus took time to look at Malchus. He was holding his head in agony, as blood streamed through his hands. Jesus, having compassion for the hurting man, reached out and returned the ear of Malchus to its rightful place.

With this action, Jesus left us a perfect example.

"Do good to them that hate you." (Matthew 5:44)

He both preached it and practiced it.

"The Son of man came not to be ministered unto, but ***to minister***." (Mark 10:45)

Even during His arrest, His heart and His hand reached out to help another who had a need. During the mockery of His trial, He was forsaken, and even denied by His cursing disciple, Peter. Yet, while angry accusers surrounded Him, He took time to turn and look upon Peter.

Luke wrote about it. As Peter vehemently denied that He even knew Jesus, "... immediately, while he yet spake, the cock crew. ***And the Lord turned, and looked upon Peter***. And Peter remembered the word of the Lord, how he had said unto him, before the cock crow, thou shalt deny me thrice. And Peter went out, and wept bitterly." (Luke 22:60-62)

That one look caused Peter to see something in Jesus' eyes that caused him to weep bitter tears. His heart was broken, for he had hurt the Lord he loved. Jesus was not as concerned about His own trial, as He was about a backslidden disciple.

Later, Jesus was beaten viciously, and His beard was pulled from His face. He was stripped; crowned with piercing thorns; and a heavy cross was flung across His torn back.

As He walked to His death, women walked along the road, weeping for Him. Jesus was more concerned about them, than He was about Himself.

"Daughters of Jerusalem," He said, turning to them, "weep not for me, but weep for yourselves, and for your children." (Luke 23:28)

Are you crying only for yourself? Do you want others to cry for you? Jesus, our Example, would not allow self-pity to consume Him with bitterness.

"***Weep not for me.***"

The spikes were driven through His flesh, and the cross lowered into its hole with a thud that jarred His bleeding body. The crosses of two thieves were placed on each side of Him. The thieves began to sneer at Him and mock His claim of being the Son of God.

"If thou be Christ, save thyself and us!" one cried.

But something stopped the sneers of the other thief.

"We receive the due reward of our deeds," he said to the other thief, "but this man hath done nothing amiss."

"Lord," he said to the One hanging beside him,

"Remember me when thou comest into thy kingdom."

Jesus again lay aside His own agony to look upon a thief, whose sins He was bearing. And He had compassion on him.

"Verily I say unto thee, Today shalt thou be with me in paradise." (Luke 23:43)

He looked down through swollen eyes and saw mockers sneering at His feet. He pitied them, for they were people with needs that they were not even aware of themselves.

"Father," He prayed. "Forgive them; for they know not what they do." (Luke 23:34)

Jesus was more concerned for His enemies than He was for Himself.

Death was almost upon Him now. The Psalmist looked ahead and described what Jesus felt that dark day. "I am poured out like water, and all my bones are out of joint: my heart is like wax; it is melted in the midst of my bowels. My strength is dried up ... my tongue cleaveth to my jaws." (Psalm 22:14-15)

Just before Jesus laid down His life, He looked down with eyes blurred by pain. He saw His mother, with John standing beside her.

"Woman," He said. "Behold thy son."

He then turned to John, and gave His mother's care to him, with these words: "Behold thy mother." (John 19:26-27)

Minutes before His torturous death, Jesus was more concerned about His mother's welfare, than His own agony.

Jesus literally moved with compassion.

He suffered obediently, so He could minister salvation to us.

You may be suffering, so you can minister healing and salvation to someone else. Jesus left you an example of looking beyond your own needs. Look around you, to the needs of others.

"As Jesus passed by, **_He saw_**."

Ask Him to open your eyes, so you will begin to see the needs of those around you.

Jesus said to Paul: "My grace is sufficient for thee: for my strength is made perfect in weakness."

Paul answered Jesus: "Most gladly will I rather glory in my infirmities (illnesses) that the power of Christ may rest upon me." (II Corinthians 12:9-10)

If you have asked God to heal you, but you are still sick, then minister to others – **_as you are_**.

God made you. God knows you. God has the hairs of your head numbered. Psalm 103:13-14 says: "Like as a father pitieth his children, so the Lord pitieth them that fear him. For he knoweth our frame; he remembereth that we are dust. Nay, but, O man, who art thou that repliest against God? Shall the thing formed say to him that formed it, Why hast thou made me thus? Shall the thing framed say of him that framed it, He had no understanding?" (Romans 9:20 and Isaiah 29:16)

Jesus ministered - **from a cross**.

Joni ministers - **from her wheelchair**.

Lester had no legs or sight, but he ministered with the one thing he had left – **his voice**.

Years ago, we attended an all-night gospel singing in an outdoor stadium, in Maumee, Ohio. We thoroughly enjoyed the beautiful music by the Blackwood Brothers and the many other groups who sang that evening.

But it wasn't until a young man began to sing a solo that our hearts were moved and tears poured from nearly every face.

His voice wasn't spectacular. We don't recall his name. Someone said that he was twenty-six years old. But his song changed at least one life that night.

He was wheeled to the organ in his wheelchair. He had no legs.

Steel arms protruded from his sleeves, as he played the organ – with no arms.

He was a human torso, with no limbs. But he used what remained of his body to glorify Jesus, his Savior.

For the first time that night, a hush settled over the entire stadium. The Holy Spirit was present, and all listened intently to a sweet voice singing these words:

> **Jesus, use me. Lord, please don't refuse me.**
> **Surely there's a work that I can do.**
> **And even though it's humble,**
> **Help my will to crumble.**
> **Though the cost be great, I'll work for You.**

Jesus did use him.

There was a work for him to do that no other person with a whole body could have accomplished.

"Lord," I prayed, as he sang, "He has no arms! He has no legs! I have both, yet I have said 'No' to You over and over again. I say, 'I can't', when You tell me to do something for You. It doesn't matter if I am not good enough! I can still do my best for You! I have legs! I have arms! Lord, please change my 'I can'ts' to 'Yes, Lord! I will! Help me!'"

His song still ministers to me. Every time I feel inferior to play, sing, teach, or write, I remember that I have arms, hands, and legs. I will use them to the best of my ability for God.

Years have passed since I heard him sing, but I thank God today for the courageous young man who used his partial body to glorify his Savior, and to bless thousands through his ministry.

We have had contact with many of the singers who sang that night. We have asked, "Do you remember a young man singing in a concert in Maumee, Ohio…" and they excitedly interrupt to tell how they will never forget him. I am not the only one who remembers vividly the lesson God taught us, as one of His choice servants played a few notes on an organ and sang *Jesus, Use Me*.

You may not remember the name, Fanny Crosby, but you will remember some of the beautiful hymns she wrote. Among the many are *Blessed Assurance; Pass Me Not, O Gentle Saviour; Jesus Is Tenderly Calling You Home; Praise Him, Praise Him; Rescue the Perishing; To God Be the Glory; He Hideth My Soul; I Am Thine, O Lord; Near the Cross*; and *Tell Me the Story of Jesus*.

Because some publishers were hesitant to have so many hymns by one person in their hymnals, Crosby used nearly 200 different names.

At the age of eight, Crosby wrote her first poem, which described her condition. For Frances Jane Crosby was blind. As a child, she remarked: "It seemed intended by the blessed providence of God that I should be blind all my life, and I thank him for the dispensation. If perfect earthly sight were offered me tomorrow I would not accept it. I might not have sung hymns to the praise of God if I had been distracted by the beautiful and interesting things about me."

She was yet a child, when she penned these words: "When I get to heaven, the first face that shall ever gladden my sight will be that of my Savior".

God used this blind woman to see beyond the beauties of earth, and into the heart of God.

Could God be using your sickness to put you in a position to minister to others who are sick, and to minister, in a more powerful way, to those who are well?

Perhaps your suffering is making you more compassionate toward others who are enduring similar trials. Seldom do we feel the pain another feels, until we have been through that pain ourselves. A sickness can open up a whole new area of ministry for you.

Perhaps you have judged and condemned others who are sick. You may have claimed that if they had your faith, they would not be sick.

Many Christians believe that anyone who is sick is either full of sin or empty of faith. They arrive at the bedside of the sick, not with sympathy or compassionate prayers, but to attack with blame!

Their belief is not new. It is as old as the book of Job. Job's friends were men who held to this teaching. Their visit to Job was a poor comfort to him. They accused Job of secret sins, and they made his days even more miserable.

"Who ever perished, being innocent?" they asked. (Job 4:7)

"Is not thy wickedness great and thine iniquities infinite?" was another accusation. (Job 22:5)

"Oh, that God would speak, and open his lips against thee," they sighed piously. "God exacteth of thee less than thine iniquity deserveth!" (Job 11:5-6)

They were implying that Job was so wicked that his punishment of the sudden loss of his family, his wealth, his servants, and his health was not severe enough!

They preached to him about the negative words he spoke. "Thine own mouth condemneth thee, and...thine own lips testify against thee." (Job 15:6)

Their condemning words did not cease. "They that plow iniquity, and sow wickedness, reap the same." (Job 4:8)

Job's accusers described him as an evil sinner, filled with iniquity.

Their opinion was far different than God's. Job 1:1 & 8 says: "There was a man in the land of Uz, whose name was Job; and **that man was perfect and upright**, and **one that feared God, and eschewed evil**. And the LORD said unto Satan, Hast thou considered my servant Job, that there is none like him in the earth, **a perfect and an upright man**, one that **feareth God**, and **escheweth** (flees and abstains from) **evil**?"

Job had heard enough accusations from his friends. Can you hear his anger in his reply to them? "No doubt but ye are the people, and wisdom shall die with you. I am not inferior to you: yea, who knoweth not such things as these? **If your soul were in my soul's stead, I** *could heap up words against you*, and shake mine head at you! *Miserable comforters* are ye all. How long will ye vex my soul, and break me in pieces with words?" (Job 19:2)

He finally gave up arguing with them.

"Mock on," he sighed wearily. (Job 21:3)

Job's "friends" went to him in his time of confusion, pain, and need. They brought their condemning and accusing attitude with them, and the Lord was not pleased with their visit to His sick servant.

God said to Eliphaz: "My wrath is kindled against thee, and against thy two friends: for **ye have not spoken of me the thing that is right.** Go to my servant Job ... and my servant Job shall pray for you: for him will I accept." (Job 42:7-8)

If you have been critical toward the sick and have judged them for what you have called their lack of faith or unconfessed sins, God may be allowing you to be sick to change you into an effective and loving witness to those who need your love and comfort.

"Who art thou that judgest another man's servant?" the Scriptures ask. "To his own master he standeth or falleth. But why dost thou judge thy brother? Or why dost thou set at nought thy brother? For we shall all stand before the judgment seat of Christ. Let us not therefore judge one another any more. Judge not, that ye be not judged. For with what judgment ye judge, ye shall be judged." (Romans 14:4, 10, 13 and Matthew 7:1-2)

If you have judged the sick, you may now be the sick one being judged by others.

Jesus did not minister judgment to the sick. He ministered love, compassion, mercy, healing, and comfort.

He expects His servants to do the same.

You may be temporarily sick to make you less judgmental and more loving toward others.

If you have been judgmental, confess your sin to God.

"Humble yourselves in the sight of the Lord, and he shall lift you up." (James 4:10)

"In lowliness of mind let each esteem other better than themselves." (Philippians 2:3)

You may be sick because you have not been faithful in a ministry to the sick. God may have placed you among the sick to minister His love and salvation.

Be faithful to your call.

Ask God to help you look beyond your own needs and see the needs of those around you. Then ask God to help you to minister His love to them.

Your sickness is only temporary. All sicknesses of the children of God are temporary. God may heal you, as He healed Job, after He has taught you things and drawn you closer to Him. Or He may heal you when you pass through the portals of death and look upon your Savior's face. He will clothe you with a new celestial body that can never be corrupted or feel pain.

Be faithful until your healing. Love God with all your heart! Keep your faith in Him! And be faithful to others!

Minister – *just as you are* – to your family, your visitors, your nurses, your doctors, the cleaning staff, and your companions in sickness. Minister with a smile, an encouraging word, an uncomplaining, loving attitude, and a testimony of unshakable faith in your Father who loves you.

Make the words of the following song *your* prayer. Let them become a sincere prayer from *your* heart.

Jesus, use me. Please Lord, don't refuse me.
Surely there's a work that I can do.
And even though it's humble,
Help my will to crumble.
Though the cost be great, I'll work for You.

Examine Yourself

- Are you as concerned about the needs of others as you should be?
- Are you one who comforts them in love?
- God is more concerned about the way you treat others, than the way you feel. If God can change you from an unfeeling, self-centered person into a loving, effective, compassionate witness through a sickness – *He will*.
- Yield to what God is doing in your life.

Obey God's two greatest commandments:

1. **"Thou shalt love the Lord thy God with all thy heart, and with all thy soul, and with all thy mind."**
2. **"Thou shalt love thy neighbor as thyself."** (Matthew 22:37 & 39)

Pray that God will remove all self-centeredness from you. Ask Him to replace it with the compassion that moved Jesus to minister to those around Him – *even from a cross.*

Remember the words of our Master to those who would follow in His steps: "Take up **your cross**, and **follow me**."

It is hard to think of the needs of others, when our own needs are great.

In fact, our self-centeredness makes it impossible – without God's help.

Jesus did it. And He can do it – *through you*.

His Word says, "Christ *in you*, the hope of glory." (Colossians 1:27)

Jesus wants to minister to the sick – this time, *through you*.

If you don't believe that this chapter applies to you, the next reason may be your answer. You may be one who is under a – **DEVIL ATTACK**.

Reason 4

DEVIL ATTACK

The description Jesus gave us of the devil is an ugly one.

"He was a **murderer** from the beginning. He is a **liar**, and the father of it. The **thief** cometh ...to **steal**, and to **kill**, and to **destroy**." (John 8:44 + 10:10)

He is further described as:

- a tempter (Matthew 4:3)
- one who deceiveth the whole world (Revelation 12:9)
- the accuser of our brethren (Revelation 12:10)
- one having great wrath (Revelation 12:12)
- the old serpent (Revelation 12:9)
- our adversary (I Peter 5:8)
- a roaring lion, walking about, seeking whom he may devour (I Peter 5:8)

Who is this enemy of ours?

God's Word records a terrible war that took place in the heavens. We need to know about it, because it directly affects each one of us.

"There was war in heaven: Michael and his angels fought against the dragon; and the dragon fought and his angels, and prevailed not; neither was their place found any more in heaven. And the great dragon was cast out, that old serpent, called the Devil, and Satan, which deceiveth the whole world: he was cast out *into the earth*, and his angels were cast out with him." (Revelation 12:7-9)

Jesus witnessed Satan's fall. "I beheld Satan as lightning fall from heaven," He told His disciples. (Luke 10:18)

Then came this warning from heaven: "**Woe** to the **inhabiters of the earth** and of the sea! For *the devil is come down unto you*, having great wrath, because he knoweth that he hath but a short time."

How can we overcome our fierce enemy?

"And they overcame him by the blood of the Lamb, and by the word of their testimony: and they loved not their lives unto the death." (Revelation 12: 11-12)

This destroyer is man's worst enemy.

He especially despises Christians, as Jesus gave us power to resist him.

The Bible warns us that "the dragon was wroth ... and went to make war with the ... seed which keep the commandments of God, and have the testimony of Jesus Christ." (Revelation 12:17)

The Bible also reveals that this adversary affects the lives of men.

Paul was one who was acquainted with Satan's methods of warfare, for he said, "we are not ignorant of his devices." (II Corinthians 2:11)

Today, many are ignorant of the devil's devices, and they unknowingly play right into his hand.

We read in Hosea 4:6 and Isaiah 5:13: "My people are destroyed for lack of knowledge. My people are gone into captivity, because they have no knowledge."

We need to know the Scriptures.

We need to know our God.

We need to know the provisions God has given us to fight our adversary.

One of the first things that a nation will do when preparing for war is to learn the tactics and the weapons of the enemy. We need to learn the methods the devil uses to try to destroy us.

God cursed the serpent in the Garden of Eden. He said: "**Dust shalt thou eat** all the days of thy life." (Genesis 3:14)

God's words to Adam were "**dust** thou art." (Genesis 3:19)

David wrote of God: "He knoweth our frame; he remembereth that **we are dust**." (Psalm 103:14)

Man is dust. The serpent's food is dust.

The serpent's food is thus ... *man*.

I Peter 5:8 says "the devil walketh about, seeking whom he may *devour (eat)*." (I Peter 5:8)

God asked Satan when he came before Him, "Whence comest thou?" Satan answered, "From going to and fro in the earth, and from walking up and down in it." (Job 1:7)

The devil's full-time business is to walk about this earth, devouring men. He has no ethics or morals. He will stoop to any means to destroy a person. Jesus called him a murderer.

He is referred to as Abaddon, in the Hebrew tongue, and Apollyon, in the Greek tongue (Revelation 9:11). Both words simply mean *destroyer*.

When people destroy themselves, the devil has

implanted the idea of suicide into their minds and convinced them to carry it out. The Bible gives us examples of suicide by weapons, drowning, hanging, and jumping from high places.

Satan is directly involved in each one.

Saul could have been a great king. He was God's choice, and anointed by Him for service. But he disobeyed God's Word.

The Bible says of him: "The spirit of the Lord departed from Saul, and an **evil spirit** from the Lord troubled him." (I Samuel 16:14)

Saul's walk with God ceased.

His walk with the devil – and trouble - began.

Saul's personality began to change.

His love for David turned to murderous hatred.

Rather than consulting God when he needed counsel, he turned to a witch for advice.

The evil spirit in Saul gained more control over him.

He confessed his inner turmoil to Samuel: "I am sore distressed." (I Samuel 28:15)

The devil finally led Saul to his final act.

"Therefore Saul took a sword, and fell upon it." (I Samuel 31:4)

The destroyer caused Saul to commit suicide … **by a weapon**.

Judas was the disciple who turned into a betrayer. But it was not Judas' idea to betray Jesus. It was Satan's. John 13:2 says: "The devil … put into the heart of Judas Iscariot … to betray him."

After completing his terrible act of betrayal, Judas hanged himself. (See Matthew 27:5) Just before he committed suicide, we read in Luke 22:3: "Then entered Satan into Judas."

The destroyer caused Judas to commit suicide - *by hanging*.

Jesus cast devils out of a wild man who spent his days in a cemetery, raging, screaming, and cutting himself with stones. He had compassion on the tormented man, and commanded the devils to leave.

"And all the devils besought him, saying, Send us into the swine, that we may enter into them. And forthwith Jesus gave them leave. And the unclean spirits went out, and entered into the swine: and the herd ran violently down a steep place into the sea, (they were about two thousand) and were choked in the sea." (Mark 5:12-13)

Even hogs were driven by the destroyer to commit suicide - *by drowning*.

The devil even dared to tempt God's own Son, Jesus. "... the devil taketh him up into the holy city, and setteth him on a pinnacle of the temple, and saith unto him, If thou be the Son of God, *cast thyself down*." (Matthew 4:5-6)

These are the words of a destroyer – daring Jesus Himself to commit suicide – *by jumping from a high place.*

Today, the destroyer is still using all these same methods to murder men. He has recently added new ones: anorexia nervosa (voluntary starvation) and bulimia nervosa. He has painted a picture of glamour, especially to the young, of a skinny body. Many girls have literally starved themselves to death, in an attempt to look "beautiful". They now lie in the grave where the destroyer has put them.

Suicide – *by starvation*.

It was the devil who was determined to destroy Job. He sent enemies, fire, and a great wind as his weapons. He stirred up men to destroy Job's servants, oxen, asses, and camels. He used a fire from the sky to burn up all Job's sheep and shepherds.

Job's sons and daughters were all in one house together the day the devil sent a great wind that destroyed the house and killed Job's ten children.

Then the devil began to destroy Job's body with sickness. He attacked Job from the crown of his head to the soles of his feet.

The devil is
    a destroyer.
        a murderer.
            our adversary.

He attacked Peter's mother-in-law with a great fever. "And Simon's wife's mother was taken with a great fever... and he (Jesus) stood over her, and **rebuked** the fever; and it left her: and immediately she arose and ministered unto them." (Luke 4:38-39)

A rebuke is a sharp reproof; an authoritative expression of disapproval. A rebuke is only given to one who is doing wrong. The destroyer was clearly involved in this woman's sickness.

Jesus was teaching on the Sabbath day in the synagogue, when a woman was brought before Him. She was a pitiful sight. Disease had ravaged her body for eighteen years, and had left her twisted, bent, and deformed. She could no longer even lift her head. Her stooped back forced her to gaze downward.

Jesus looked tenderly at this broken woman, and called her to Him.

"Woman, thou art loosed from thine infirmity." He said, as He laid His hands on her twisted body. The congregation watched in awe as her crooked body was immediately made straight. The Bible tells us that they glorified God.

The ruler of the synagogue (who was more concerned about order in the service than with the woman who desperately needed healing) was irate. He accused Jesus of working on the Sabbath day, and informed Him that there were six other days He could perform His miracles! (Perhaps he would not have felt that way if it had been himself or his wife who had been deformed.)

Jesus addressed him as a hypocrite, then asked, "Ought not this woman, **whom *Satan hath bound*, lo, these *eighteen years*,** be ***loosed from this bond*** on the Sabbath day?" (Luke 13:12-13 & 16)

The religious ruler of the synagogue desired to restrict Jesus' time to deliver devil oppressed people, to just six days a week.

Many religious rulers of our day teach their congregations that Jesus' power to deliver the devil oppressed is limited to the past – for another time, and for another generation. They too desire to restrict Christ's power to set the captive free.

But Jesus ***was*** – and ***is*** – always ready to set anyone free who is bound by the power of Satan. The critical bystanders could not stop Him from setting captives free then – and they cannot stop Him now. He is still setting people free from evil spirits today.

"Then was brought unto him one **possessed with a devil**, **blind, and dumb**: and he healed him, insomuch that the blind and dumb both spake and saw." (Matthew 12:22)

Matthew 9:32-33 tells us that "they brought to him a dumb man possessed with a devil. And **when the devil was cast out**, the **dumb spake**."

A father brought his son to Jesus. Kneeling before Him, he pleaded, "Lord, have mercy on my son: for he is lunatic (insane), and sore vexed: for ofttimes he falleth into the fire, and oft into the water. And Jesus **rebuked the devil**; and he departed out of him: and the child was cured from that very hour." (Matthew 17:15, 18)

Peter preached: "God anointed Jesus of Nazareth with the Holy Ghost and with power: who went about doing good, and **healing all that were oppressed of the devil**." (Acts 10:38)

The devil takes pleasure in destroying. He destroys human bodies. He also afflicts Christians, in the hope of destroying their faith in God's love.

Satan longed to change Job's worship of God into curses against God.

Jesus told Peter: "Simon, Simon, behold, **Satan hath desired to have you**, that he may sift you as wheat: but I have prayed for thee, that **thy faith fail not**." (Luke 22:31-32)

If your sickness is causing your faith in God to waver and to doubt God's love for you, the devil has accomplished his diabolical purpose. When your faith in God is weakened, you are wide open to Satan's attack.

Our faith in God is our shield. Ephesians 6:16 is a warning to us: "Above all, taking the **shield of faith**, wherewith ye shall be able to **quench all the *fiery darts of the wicked***."

Peter warned us, "Be sober, be vigilant; because **your adversary the devil**, as a roaring lion, walketh about, **seeking whom he may devour**: whom **resist** steadfast in the **faith**, knowing that the same afflictions (pains; sufferings; distresses) are accomplished in your brethren that are in the world." (I Peter 5:8-9)

Satan still attacks God's servants to keep them from ministering to others.

Peter's mother-in-law lay in bed with a raging fever, perhaps knowing that Jesus was on His way to her house. She would have wanted to prepare for His visit, but Satan had rendered her useless. After Jesus rebuked the fever, the Bible says, "and immediately she arose and ministered unto them." (Luke 4:39)

Perhaps you are one of God's children who sincerely desires to labor in God's harvest field, but your sickness has kept you from serving.

There is good news for you! There is One who is a greater **DESTROYER** than the devil!

I John 3:8 tells us: "**For this purpose** the Son of God was manifested, that he might **DESTROY** the works of the devil!"

Wherever Jesus went, He destroyed the devil's works!

He **healed** those who Satan had attacked with sickness!

He **cleansed** those who Satan had tempted to sin!

He **delivered** those who were bound by Satan!

He **brought life** to those who Satan had killed with spiritual death!

Hebrews 2:14 says that "... through death he (Jesus) might **DESTROY HIM** that had the power of **death**, that is, **the devil**!"

Jesus told His seventy disciples, "I give unto **you** power to tread on serpents and scorpions, and **over all the power of the enemy**!" (Luke 10:19)

Psalm 91:13 says: "Thou shalt tread upon the lion and adder: the young lion and the **dragon** shalt thou trample under feet."

Who is this dragon?

Revelation 12:9 identifies him: "The **great dragon** ... that *old serpent*, called the **Devil**, and **Satan**, which deceiveth the whole world."

That old serpent had been in Eden, seducing Eve to disobey God.

The Apostle Paul was attacked by Satan, but he left us an example of victory.

He had just escaped a shipwreck and was on an island with the other survivors. It was cold and raining, and their clothes were soaked. The natives built their visitors a fire to warm them.

Paul gathered sticks to keep the fire going. When he was placing them on the fire, "there came a viper out of the heat, and fastened on his hand. And he shook off the beast into the fire, and felt no harm.

"Howbeit (the natives) looked when he should have swollen, or fallen down dead suddenly: but after they had looked a great while ... saw no harm come to him." (Acts 28:3 & 5-6)

There were 276 shipwrecked survivors on the island. The natives were gathered around them. The devil chose one man to attack - Paul!

Paul had boldly marched into Satan's kingdom, and had turned many to Christ. The devil's attack was vicious. He had failed in his attempt to drown Paul by wrecking the ship, so he used a viper. But Paul merely shook the snake off. He *resisted* the power of Satan.

James 4:7 tells believers: "Submit yourselves therefore to God." (Paul had done this.) "**Resist the devil**, and *he will flee* from you."

Are you fully submitted to God? Has the devil attacked you spiritually, mentally, or physically? **Resist him**! Cast him away from you, for God's Word assures us that he will literally run! There is power in the name of JESUS – but only if you use it! He told us to use His name freely to cast away the devil and the afflictions that come from his attacks.

Among Jesus' last words to His disciples were: "These signs shall follow them that believe; in my name shall they cast out devils." (Mark 16:17)

Jesus said, "**All** power is given unto me in heaven and in earth." (Matthew 28:18)

God tells us to be "strong in the Lord, and in the *power of his might*. **Put on the whole armour of God, that ye may be able to stand against the wiles of the devil**. For we **wrestle** not against flesh and blood, but against principalities, against powers, against the rulers of the darkness of this world, against spiritual wickedness in high places. Wherefore take unto you the **whole armour of God**, that ye may be able to **_withstand_** in the evil day, and having done all, to **stand**!" (Ephesians 6:10-13)

You must **stand** against this enemy!

And you must **_withstand_** him!

It is easy for a house to stand. But when a powerful tornado roars against it, it needs to be strong enough to withstand its force.

You may have been standing easily while you were healthy. But are you withstanding the enemy's attack? God has provided a suit of armour for you to wear, so you can withstand your vicious enemy.

But if **fear** drives out your **faith** and causes you to turn your back to the devil and run — you are in trouble. There is no protection for your back, because the Lord has told you to stand boldly and **resist** the devil.

The devil will then flee from you, for there is power in the name of Jesus. The Psalmist said, "**Through thy name** will we **_tread them under_** that **rise up against us**." (Psalm 44:5)

The battle is fierce.

The same Paul, who shook the viper from his hand, later wrote to the Thessalonians: "Wherefore we would have come unto you, even I **Paul, once and again; but Satan hindered us**." (I Thessalonians 2:18)

Has Satan hindered you from victoriously serving the Lord?

Has he nearly defeated you with sickness? Is he destroying your ability to serve God effectively?

Has he weakened your faith in your loving Father?

Paul was concerned "lest Satan should get an advantage of us." (II Corinthians 2:11)

God never told us to ignore the devil. He told us to resist him.

Jesus battled the devil. "Then was Jesus led up of the Spirit into the wilderness to be tempted of the devil."

During His temptation, He repeatedly said to the devil, "It is written …" (Matthew 4:4, 7 & 10)

Then He used the truth of God's Word to defeat Satan's lies. And Matthew 4:10 tells us: "Then the **devil leaveth** him."

Jesus first submitted to His Father.
Then He resisted the devil.
Then the devil left.

Conclusion

Paul wrote Timothy that he was concerned that men "may recover themselves out of the snare of the devil, who are taken captive by him at his will." (II Timothy 2:26)

This is speaking of unbelievers. But the devil has no right to take the child of God captive.

He may – and will attack us. But we are told to resist him, rather than passively accepting his darts and collapsing in defeat.

Ephesians 4:27 commands us to "neither give place to the devil."

Have you allowed him to take possession of part of your body and destroy it through sickness?

Don't give him even one place! Fight him with the Sword of the Spirit! Keep your Shield of Faith ready to quench every dart of fire coming from the mouth of the dragon.

Paul ended his life with these triumphant words:

* I have **fought** a good fight!
* I have **finished** my course!
* I have **kept** the faith! (II Timothy 4:7)

Submit to God!
Resist the devil!
Then – and only then – he must flee.

You Can Resist the Devil

Jesus spoke to the devil, and commanded him with authority and power to leave peoples' bodies. When He ascended to heaven, He left His followers with the power and authority to use His name.

If you believe that your sickness may be an attack by Satan, resist the enemy, in the powerful name of Jesus. According to Ephesians 6:11, the only way to stand against the wiles of the devil is to put on the whole armour of God. What is this armour that God has provided for us? It is described in Ephesians 6:14-16.

We are to have our loins girt about with **TRUTH**. **Truth** is the weapon that fights lies! Settle it in your heart – **God speaks truth**. Jesus said, in John 14:6, that He *is* Truth.

Put on the Breastplate of **RIGHTEOUSNESS**. When you allow Jesus to live *in* and *through* you – you will *have* righteousness, and you will *be* righteous. Sin cannot penetrate the Breastplate of Righteousness.

Put the **GOSPEL OF PEACE** on your feet! A multitude of angels came from heaven to sing Jesus' birth announcement to the shepherds. Luke 2:14 records their song: "Glory to God in the highest, and on earth **peace**, good will *toward* men." They did not announce that there would be peace *among* men. But, because of Jesus' birth, death, and resurrection, we now can have peace **with** God! The Peacemaker descended *from* God *toward* us!

"On earth peace – *toward* men!"

The Bible tells us "that he might reconcile both unto God in one body by the cross, having slain the enmity thereby: and came and *preached peace* to you which were afar off, and to them that were nigh." (Ephesians 2:16-17)

II Corinthians 5:18 tells us that God has reconciled us to Himself by Jesus Christ. Jesus brought peace *between God and man* by His dying in our place, as judgment for our sins. Isaiah 9:6 calls Him the "**Prince of Peace**."

When we have received Jesus as our Savior, we are at peace with God. Galatians 5:25 tells us that "If we live in the Spirit, let us also *walk* in the Spirit".

"Stand therefore, having ... your feet shod with the preparation of the gospel of peace."

If you are not wearing peace as you walk this Christian life, you do not have on the whole armour of God. The

Gospel of Peace protects you from being condemned to hell. The Gospel of Peace protects you from hatred, unforgiveness, grudges, and bitterness toward others.

Pick up your shield! It is made entirely of **FAITH**! Never allow anything or anyone to destroy your faith in God and His love for you. How the devil must have cringed when Job said from his pain-wracked body: "For I know that my redeemer liveth, and that he shall stand at the latter day upon the earth: and though after my skin worms destroy this body, yet in my flesh shall I see God: Whom I shall see for myself, and mine eyes shall behold, and not another; though my reins be consumed within me." (Job 19:25-27) The devil himself could not penetrate Job's shield of faith!

Have you put on your Helmet of **SALVATION**? Do you believe that God has provided His only begotten Son to save you from your sins? Have you been to the cross of Calvary? Have you seen Jesus, the Sacrifice for your sins, hanging there – simply because He loves you?
Have you confessed your sins, and asked Him to save your soul? Have you asked Him to cleanse you with His blood? Have you invited Him into your heart, by faith? Is He now living in and through you? Unless you are saved, you have no helmet!

Have you picked up your sword? It is the **WORD OF GOD**! Jesus used this sword when He fought the devil in the wilderness. He quoted Scriptures that answered every temptation with: **"It is written..."**

Are you **PRAYING always**, with all prayer and supplication in the Spirit?

You will never be able to resist the devil in your own power. God provided a full armour for one reason. You need it, in order to withstand the enemy's blows.

Examine Yourself

Perhaps you are still unsure why you are sick. Continue to seek an answer, as you read the following chapter. None of us want to admit it, but the cause of your suffering may be - **SIN**.

Reason 5

SIN

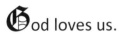od loves us.

His love rings from the pages of Genesis to Revelation. His love created us for His pleasure.

His love placed us in a world of beauty with flowers and trees, lakes and streams, animals and birds, sunsets and beautiful stars.

His love kept Him silent when His only begotten Son was brutally whipped and cruelly displayed on a wooden cross, so we could have salvation.

As much as God loves us, **God hates sin**. It was as much hate that drove Jesus to the cross, as it was love. If God did not hate sin, there would have been no reason for Jesus to die. I John 3:5 tells us that Jesus "was manifested to **take away our sins**."

The Psalmist looked forward to the Messiah's coming, and prophesied of Him: "He shall redeem their soul from deceit and violence" (Psalm 72:14).

The angel descended to explain to Joseph that Mary would bring God's Son into the world, and spoke these words: "And she shall bring forth a son, and thou shalt call his name JESUS: for he shall *save his people* **from their sins**" (Matthew 1:21).

Why does God hate sin? Does His hatred of sin change God from One of love to One of hate? No! Rather, it is His matchless love for His creation that causes Him to hate **sin**!

The more one loves, the greater he hates the thing that harms the one he loves!

A mother, who loves her child, hates anything that threatens his safety and happiness. A father hates the drug that is destroying the mind of his addicted teenager. A wife hates the alcohol that transforms her loving husband into a heartless beast. A husband, who loved his wife, hates the nicotine that ravaged her lungs and took her away from him prematurely.

Should it not then be easily understood why our God, who lovingly created man and fashioned a beautiful world for him, hates the sin that destroys bodies, minds, and souls?

Sin has ravaged God's creation. Its wage is death. It reverses the perfect creation of God, by torturing, maiming, crippling, and mocking God's handiwork with chaotic destruction.

Today, many have lost sight of the fact that God hates sin. Our modern day concept of God is of an indulgent Father who smiles down upon us; turns His head and covers His eyes when we sin; and never disciplines or frowns on our disobedience and rebellion. He heaps blessings upon us, even when we ignore His command-ments. We become so spoiled, that our prayers most often consist of complaints and begging for more possessions.

This portrait of God is popular – **but it is false**. This is not the timeless, true God of the Scriptures.

Paul warned the church: "But I fear, lest by any means, as the serpent beguiled Eve through his subtilty, so your minds should be corrupted from the simplicity that is in Christ. For if he that cometh preacheth *another Jesus*, whom we have not preached, or if ye receive *another spirit*, which ye have not received, or *another gospel*, which ye have not accepted, ye might well bear with him."

Don't bear (stand for – put up with – endure) anyone who comes preaching *any other Jesus* than the One preached by the apostles; *any other Spirit*, than the Holy Spirit who authored the Word of God; or *any other gospel*, than the gospel Jesus sent His disciples out to preach!

God demands our obedience. His Word states: "Let us hear the conclusion of the whole matter: Fear God, and *keep his commandments*: for this is the *whole duty of man.* For God shall bring every work into judgment, with every secret thing, whether it be good, or whether it be evil" (Ecclesiastes 12:13-14).

Does God demand our obedience?

Let Him answer.

"He that saith, I know him, and **keepeth not his commandments**, is a **liar**, and the truth is not in him." (I John 2:4).

Does God see our sins? Many preachers claim He doesn't. But what does God say?

"The eyes of the Lord are in every place, beholding the evil and the good" (Proverbs 15:3).

Will God bless us, as we sin?

He answers: "Your sins have withholden good things from you" (Jeremiah 5:25).

Can we hide our sins from Him?

"Be sure your sin will find you out. They are not hid

from my face, neither is their iniquity hid from mine eyes" (Numbers 32:23 and Jeremiah 16:17).

Can we hide from God when we sin?

Again, let the Lord answer this question. "Can any hide himself in secret places that I shall not see him? saith the Lord. Do not I fill heaven and earth? saith the Lord" (Jeremiah 23:24).

Will God judge sin?

"Marvel not at this:" Jesus said, "for the hour is coming, in the which all that are in the graves shall hear his voice, and shall come forth; they that have done good, unto the resurrection of life; and they that have done evil, unto the resurrection of damnation. Vengeance belongeth unto me, I will recompense, saith the Lord. And again, *the Lord shall judge his people*" (John 5:28-29 and Hebrews 10:30).

Will God punish Christians – His own children – when they do wrong?

God answers: "My son, despise not thou the chastening of the Lord, nor faint when thou art rebuked of him: for whom the Lord loveth he chasteneth, and scourgeth every son whom he receiveth. If ye endure chastening, God dealeth with you as sons; for what son is he whom the father chasteneth not? But if ye be without chastisement, whereof all are partakers, then are ye bastards, and not sons" (Hebrews 12:5-8).

Perhaps you know a child whose parents have never disciplined, corrected, or withheld things from him. He is undoubtedly spoiled, proud, and greedy.

Loving parents use discipline to train their children. As a wise and loving Father, God will assuredly chastise, discipline, correct, and withhold blessings from us to perfect us.

A popular teaching in our day is that God only does things that we consider to be good. Teachers, who believe this, reject the thought that God does many things **for our good**, that do not seem good to us.

A mother will slap a child's hand when he reaches out to touch a flame. Does she do that because of her lack of love? No! She slaps him, because she loves him and knows that the pain of her slap is far less severe than the burn of the fire.

Sin brings judgment.

Judgment brings hell.

Chastisement by God now cannot even be compared to the torments of eternal hell fire in the future.

Will God sometimes use sickness to judge sin or chastise His people for their sins?

God says: "Come, and let us return unto the Lord: for **he hath torn**, and he will heal us; **he hath smitten**, and he will bind us up." (Hosea 6:1)

The Lord asked Moses: "Who hath made man's mouth? or who maketh the **dumb**, or **deaf**, or the seeing, or the **blind**? have not **I the Lord**?" (Exodus 4:11)

This does not say that dumbness, deafness, or blindness are the result of sin.

But this verse does show us that the Lord makes the deaf, dumb, and blind ... for His purpose. He is God!

I Samuel 2:6-7 says: "The Lord killeth, and maketh alive: he bringeth down to the grave, and bringeth up. The Lord maketh poor, and maketh rich: he bringeth low, and lifteth up."

Again we read the words of the Lord: "See now that I, even I, am he, and there is no god with me: I kill, and I make alive; *I wound*, and I heal: neither is there any that can deliver out of *my hand*." (Deuteronomy 32:39)

Some will contradict His Word with their arguments: "But I've been taught that only the devil causes sickness, and he is always the one who smites and wounds."

God's eternal answer is: "Nay but, O man, who art thou that repliest against God? Shall the thing formed say to him that formed it, Why hast thou made me thus? Hath not the potter power over the clay?" (Romans 9:20-21)

Truth cannot be measured by its popularity. Truth comes only from God.

And the God of the Word uses sickness for His purposes: to judge sinners and to correct His people with chastisement.

God does not need the devil to accomplish His purpose.

When God called Moses to deliver the children of Israel from captivity, He told him to put his hand into his bosom. Moses obeyed. When he brought his hand back out, it was "leprous as snow". He put it into his bosom the second time, and when he brought it out, his hand was healed. (Exodus 4:6-7)

Who struck Moses' hand with leprosy? The answer is clear. *God did*. The meeting was between God and Moses alone.

Who healed Moses' hand from leprosy? Again, the answer is clear. *God did.*

God is the One who poured plagues on Egypt. One of

them was a disease that afflicted animals.

Exodus 9:3 says: "Behold, the **hand of the Lord** is upon thy cattle which is in the field, upon the horses, upon the asses, upon the camels, upon the oxen, and upon the sheep: there shall be a very grievous murrain."

A murrain is a malignant fever that affects domestic animals.

Another plague fell when Moses obeyed God's command to throw ashes toward heaven. As the ashes rained down, great boils broke forth upon both man and beast. (See Exodus 9:8-11.)

The modern church no longer believes the words of God, recorded by Isaiah: "I am the LORD, and there is none else. I form the light, and create darkness: I make peace, and create evil: *I the LORD do all these things.*" (Isaiah 45:6-7)

When Pharaoh refused to release God's people, God continued to judge Egypt for its rebellion. The last plague happened at midnight, when "... ***the Lord smote*** all the firstborn in the land of Egypt, from the firstborn of Pharaoh that sat on his throne unto the firstborn of the captive that was in the dungeon; and all the firstborn of cattle." (Exodus 12:29)

"The Lord killeth, and maketh alive ..."

After the children of Israel were finally on their way to their promised land, Pharaoh and his army pursued them.

"...and **the Lord overthrew** the Egyptians in the midst of the sea." (Exodus 14:27)

James 4:12 teaches us that "There is one lawgiver, who is able to *save* and to *destroy*..."

God sent these plagues on the Egyptians, who were mistreating His people.

But later, when His own people began to complain because they had left Egypt, "... the wrath of the LORD was kindled against the people, and **the LORD smote the people** with a very great plague." (Numbers 11:33)

When Korah rebelled against Moses' position as leader, God literally opened up the earth and swallowed him up! See Numbers 16:30-33.

"... He bringeth down to the grave."

The people were angry then, just as many are angry today, when the God who both saves and destroys, is preached.

"But on the morrow all the congregation of the children of Israel murmured against Moses and against Aaron, saying, Ye have killed the people of the Lord! And the Lord spake unto Moses, saying, Get you up from among this congregation, that **I may consume them** as in a moment. Now they that died in the plague were fourteen thousand and seven hundred, beside them that died about the matter of Korah." (Numbers 16:41, 44, 45, 49)

God struck Ananias and Sapphira in the middle of a church service, because they claimed to have given all their money from a land sale to God, when they had only given part. (Acts 5:1-11) Their sins were lying and hypocrisy.

When people began to worship Herod as a god, and shouted at the completion of his oration: "It is the voice of a god, and not of a man," God stopped their worship. "And immediately **the angel of the Lord smote him**, because he gave not God the glory: and he was eaten of worms, and gave up the ghost." (Acts 12:22-23)

When Paul was witnessing to Sergius Paulus, Elymas, a sorcerer, interrupted him to ridicule Paul's message.

"Then Saul ... **filled with the Holy Ghost**, set his eyes on him, and said, O full of all subtility and all mischief, thou child of the devil, thou enemy of all righteousness, wilt thou not cease to pervert the right ways of the Lord? And now, behold, ***the hand of the Lord*** *is upon thee*, **and thou shalt be blind**, not seeing the sun for a season. And immediately there fell on him a mist and a darkness; and he went about seeking some to lead him by the hand." (Acts 13:9-12)

Saul was filled with the Holy Ghost, when he spoke this message to Elymas. Yet men dare to challenge the words of the Holy Ghost Himself!

We have already discussed King Nebuchadnezzar's insanity, that caused him to acknowledge God as the greatest King of all. Daniel 4:13 & 17 & 23 reveals to us that it was the watcher – **the holy one who came down from heaven** – who struck this proud king and caused him to make his residence in the field with the beasts!

It has been widely taught that God does not afflict, judge, or discipline. As a result, people no longer fear God.

Yet, God's Word says, "The fear of the Lord is the beginning of wisdom." (Psalm 111:10)

Jesus warned us: "I say unto you my friends, Be not afraid of them that kill the body, and after that have no more that they can do. But I will forewarn you whom ye shall fear: Fear him, which after he hath killed hath power to cast into hell; yea, I say unto you, Fear him." (Luke 12:4-5)

He also said, referring to Himself, "... The stone which the builders rejected, the same is become the head of the corner... and whosoever shall fall on this stone shall be broken: but on whomsoever it shall fall, **it will grind him to powder.**" (Matthew 21:42 & 44)

God has given us a choice.

We can either fall on Christ and let Him save us, cleanse us, break us, and mold us into His image, or we can refuse to receive Him as our Savior.

If we refuse His mercy, He will fall on us in judgment, and will grind us to powder.

The Psalmist said, "The Lord preserveth all them that love him: but all the wicked will *he destroy*." (Psalm 145:20)

Many refuse to see God as He is! Many are afraid to look on Him! Many have invented a god who is not the God of the Scriptures. Instead of looking at the God who made us in His image, false teachers have made themselves a god, made in man's image.

Their god gives them their every desire, smiles at their disobedience, ignores their rebellion, showers them with blessings, withholds any chastisement, winks at their sins, expects no service from them, and ushers them into heaven with rewards and a greeting of "Well done".

We need to know the true God. He is revealed in His Word. You need to know that God, in His mercy and love for you, may be the One responsible for your sickness.

In fact, our God, who is pure **LOVE**, will do anything it takes to get you to heaven instead of hell - including turning away from the anguished cries of His only begotten and beloved Son. He allowed Jesus' to die a torturous death, just to save *you*. That's how much He wants you to spend your eternity in His home, with Him.

He is more concerned about your eternal well-being and the sickness of your soul, than a temporary sickness of your body.

You and others may have asked God to heal your body. You may have had believers pray for you in healing services.

But God has not touched you and made you whole.

Perhaps the reason that you are still sick is found in these Scriptures: "Behold, the Lord's hand is not shortened, that it cannot save; neither his ear heavy, that it cannot hear: but *your iniquities have separated between you and your God, and your sins have hid his face from you, that he will not hear*." (Isaiah 59:1-2)

What Are These Sins?

Many sicknesses are the direct result of sin. Some of these are easily identified. For example, one of the causes of cirrhosis of the liver is consumption of alcohol.

There are warnings in God's Word about drunkenness. God commands us not to even look upon "... the wine when it is red, when it giveth his colour in the cup, when it moveth itself aright. At the last it biteth like a serpent, and stingeth like an adder." (Proverbs 23:31-32)

Galatians 5:19-21 clearly states that one of the works of the flesh is drunkenness. Then it adds: "And they that do such things shall not inherit the kingdom of God."

Proverbs 20:1 warns us that "wine is a mocker, strong drink is raging: and whosoever is **deceived** thereby is not wise."

Many drunkards do not recognize the **deception** of alcohol, until their livers are damaged beyond repair.

Breaking God's commandments is sin. God warns us repeatedly throughout the Scriptures against drunkenness. He does this for our good.

I John 5:3 tells us, "His commandments are **not grievous**." Obeying them does not cause grief, but disobeying them does. If one destroys his body by drinking, he has chosen to destroy his own body. Grief will be the result.

The heart cry of God is: "O that there were such an heart in them, that they would fear me, and keep **all my commandments** always, that it might be **well** with them, and with their children for ever." (Deuteronomy 5:29)

"God – why am I sick?"

If your liver was damaged by your lifestyle of drunkenness, your question is easily answered. You are sick, because you have chosen to ignore God's commandment.

Another one of God's commandments forbids adultery and fornication. Many ignore these commands, label them old-fashioned, and bring venereal disease, chancroid, gonorrhea, syphilis, or herpes on themselves.

I Corinthians 6:18 is another commandment: "Flee

fornication ... he that committeth fornication sinneth *against his own body*."

God also forbids sodomy. Men rebel. Homosexuals are so numerous in our day that they have become accepted by most of society – but not by God. God calls it vile affections, and declares that men who burn in their lust one toward another are worthy of death. (Romans 1:24-32)

Leviticus 20:13 declares emphatically: "If a man also lie with mankind, as he lieth with a woman, both of them have committed an abomination."

The Bible tells us in I Corinthians 6:9-10: "Be not deceived: neither ... effeminate, nor abusers of them- selves with mankind ... shall inherit the kingdom of God."

God destroyed two cities (Sodom and Gomorrah) because the men of those cities were homosexuals. (See Genesis 19:4-11 and Jude 1:7.)

AIDS is a disease that began its spread by those who were involved in homosexual activity.

In 2011, there were an estimated 34 million people living with HIV/AIDS in the world. In 2011 alone, 1.7 million people died of AIDS.

Since the disease was first recognized, it has caused an estimated 36 million deaths.

We need to remember that *keeping* God's command- ments does not cause grief. However, *breaking* them does.

Sin breeds sickness. James 1:15 warns: **"Sin, when it is finished, bringeth forth death."**

Smoking blackens the lungs with cancer and claims

thousands of people each year with premature death. Other victims of nicotine gasp through life with emphysema, a disease that drains energy from their bodies. Over 443,000 die from smoking *every year* in the United States alone. This is more than the total number of Americans who died in World War II – and it happens every single year! Four-million people die annually in the world from their addiction to nicotine, a form of slow suicide.

Sins of gluttony, slothfulness, and smoldering anger also cause illnesses.

We have seen the ravaging results of drugs, as they claim the brain cells of both teenagers and adults, reducing them to slaves to the drugs their bodies and minds crave.

Our generation is addicted to pills – pills to lose weight; pills to go to sleep; pills to wake up; pills to stay alert; pills to be less alert; pills to regain vitality; pills to build muscles – all combining to bring a near breakdown of the nervous system of an entire generation. We have visited many in hospitals who were near death because of the overuse and abuse of prescription drugs.

Overworking is sin. God Himself rested an entire day after working for six days to create the world. Some people feel guilty if they rest, yet God has instructed us to rest one day out of seven. We would feel better mentally, physically, and spiritually, if we used the day as God intended it to be used – as a day of rest.

"Six days shalt thou labour, and do all thy work," God commanded His people, "but the seventh day is the Sabbath of the Lord thy God: in it thou shalt not do any work." (Exodus 20:8-10)

Jesus said, "The Sabbath was made for man, and not man for the sabbath." (Mark 2:27)

The Sabbath is a day free from labor; a day for man to rest with no condemnation or guilt. By resting one day a week, men would work more productively six days.

"Come ye yourselves apart into a desert place, and rest a while," Jesus advised His disciples. (Mark 6:31)

They did. Epaphroditus didn't.

He worked for the Apostle Paul until he nearly died of sickness. The churches had not supported Paul as they should have, so Epaphroditus took the burden of Paul's support upon himself.

Paul described him to the negligent church as one who "ministered to my wants. For indeed he was *sick nigh unto death* ... because for the work of Christ he was *nigh unto death*, not regarding his life, to supply your lack of service toward me." (Philippians 2:25, 27, 30)

His work was honourable and good, but he was human.

We have a mortal body that requires sleep and rest. And this faithful servant of God nearly died, because he worked without rest.

Worry is another sin. Romans 14:23 tells us that which "... is not of faith is sin." Worry causes many sicknesses. Most physicians would trace a large percentage of their patients' illnesses directly to worry or stress.

What is worry? It is a lack of trust in our heavenly Father. Babies are not afflicted with stomach ulcers and headaches caused from anxiety. They trust their parents to care for their needs.

Jesus taught: "Take no thought, saying, What shall we eat? or, What shall we drink? or Wherewithal shall we be clothed? For your heavenly Father knoweth that ye have need of all these things. But seek ye first the kingdom of God, and his righteousness, and all these things shall be added unto you."

Then He added this advice to us: "Take no thought for the morrow: for the morrow shall take thought for the things of itself. Sufficient unto the day is the evil thereof." (Matthew 6:31-34)

How can you function effectively today, if the whole burden of tomorrow is weighing you down?

"Cast thy burden upon the Lord, and he shall sustain thee," God tells us.

"Casting all your care upon him; for he careth for you." (Psalm 55:22 and I Peter 5:7)

Replace worry with trust in God!

Turn every worry into a prayer!

Hatred and bitterness can also cause sickness. God warns us to look diligently, "lest any root of bitterness springing up trouble you, and thereby many be defiled." (Hebrews 12:15)

Sin causes sickness!

After Jesus touched a man crippled from birth, he was instantly healed. He got up and walked for the first time in his thirty-eight years! Jesus warned him, "**Sin no more**, lest *a worse thing* come unto thee." (John 5:14)

With this statement, Jesus emphasized the fact that sin does result in sickness.

James wrote, "**Confess your faults** one to another,

and pray one for another, that ye may be **healed**!" (James 5:16)

Not only will sin bring sickness directly to the body, but God will bring sickness and pain to the sinner as judgment of sin, and to the Christians as chastisement of sin. There are many examples of this in the Bible.

Elisha's servant, Gahazi, ran after Naaman's chariot after Naaman was healed of his leprosy. He lied to Naaman, claiming that Elisha had changed his mind and wanted a payment for Naaman's healing. God revealed to Elisha what Gahazi had done, and he was punished for his lie. Elisha said to Gahazi: "The leprosy therefore of Naaman shall cleave unto thee, and unto thy seed for ever. And he went out from his presence a leper as white as snow." (II Kings 5:27)

The leprosy that afflicted Gahazi and his descendants was the direct result of Gahazi's sin.

God judged Moses' sister, Miriam, with that same dreaded disease. She had rebelled against her brother's position as God's choice to lead the Israelites to the promised land.

The Lord came down to earth in the pillar of the cloud and asked Miriam, "Wherefore then were ye not afraid to speak against my servant Moses? And the anger of the Lord was kindled ... and the cloud departed from off the tabernacle; and, behold, Miriam became leprous, white as snow: and Aaron looked upon Miriam, and, behold, she was leprous." (Numbers 12:8-10)

Her sickness was the direct result of her sin.

David, the king of Israel, committed adultery with Bathsheba, the wife of Uriah, who was fighting in a war.

When David learned that Bathsheba was carrying his child, he sent orders to put Uriah in the front lines, to assure his death. David not only broke God's commandment by committing adultery, he also compounded his sin by indirectly becoming Uriah's murderer.

After David and Bathsheba's baby was born, God sent His prophet, Nathan, with this message for David: "Because by this deed thou hast given great occasion to the enemies of the Lord to blaspheme, the child also that is born unto thee shall surely die. And Nathan departed unto his house, and **the Lord struck the child** that Uriah's wife bare unto David, and **it was very sick** ... and it came to pass on the seventh day, that the child died." (II Samuel 12:14-15 & 18)

The child's sickness was a direct result of David's adultery.

God never ignores sin. You may know some people who seemingly are getting away with their sins, and who have perfectly healthy bodies.

I Timothy 5:24 says: "Some men's sins are open beforehand, going before to judgment; and some men they follow after."

One thing is sure: judgment always follows sin, if not in this life, then in the next.

God is a loving and merciful God. He gave even the wicked queen, Jezebel, a space (length of time) to repent, before He judged her for turning His people to false gods. (Revelation 2:20-21)

Queen Jezebel had heard her doom prophesied by the prophet of God, but she no doubt scoffed when God's judgment did not immediately fall. As the days and years passed by, she grew more confident in her ability to mock God and get away with it. Jezebel failed to realize that each passing day was given her by our God of mercy. He was even giving this rebellious woman a time to repent, before He judged her for her wickedness.

She scoffed her time of grace away, until the moment came that the time given to her to repent had passed. Her own servants threw her from an upper story window. The hooves of horses crushed her body, and dogs ate it.

Jezebel's day of judgment had come.

Throughout the Old Testament, God judged kings who rebelled against His laws. Jehoram was one of these. He led an entire nation to rebel against God.

"And there came a writing to him from Elijah the prophet, saying, Thus saith the Lord God of David thy father, Because thou hast not walked in the ways of Jehoshaphat thy father, nor in the ways of Asa king of Judah, but has walked in the way of the kings of Israel, and hast made Judah and the inhabitants of Jerusalem to go a whoring, like to the whoredoms of the house of Ahab, and also hast slain thy brethren of thy father's house, which were better than thyself: *behold, with a great plague will <u>the Lord smite thy people and thy children, and thy wives,</u> and all thy goods: and thou shalt have <u>great sickness</u> ... day by day*.

"And after all this <u>*the Lord smote him in his bowels with an incurable disease*</u>. And it came to pass, that in process of time, after the end of two years, his bowels fell out by reason of *his sickness*: so he died of *sore diseases*." (II Chronicles 21:12-15 & 18-19)

God declared to the Israelites, through Moses: "If thou wilt not hearken unto the voice of the Lord thy God, to observe to do all his commandments and his statues which I command thee this day; that all these curses shall come upon thee, and overtake thee. The **Lord shall smite thee** with a consumption, and with a fever, and with an inflammation, and with an extreme burning ... with the botch (boil) of Egypt, and with the emerods (tumors), and with the scab, and with the itch, whereof thou canst not be healed. The **_Lord shall smite thee_** with madness, and blindness, and astonishment of heart (heart attacks)." (Deuteronomy 28:15 & 22 & 27-28)

God promised His people that if they would "hearken to these judgments, and keep, and do them", He would then "take away from thee all sickness, and will put none of the evil diseases of Egypt, which thou knowest, upon thee."

The same God warned the same people that if they would "not observe to do all the words of this law that are written in this book," that He would "bring upon thee all the diseases of Egypt, which thou wast afraid of; and they shall cleave unto thee." (Deuteronomy 7:12 & 15 and 28:58 & 60)

After David sinned, he told God, "There is no soundness in my flesh because of thine anger; neither is there any rest in my bones *because of my sin*. For my lions are filled with a *loathsome disease*: and there is no soundness in my flesh. I am feeble and sore broken ... my strength faileth me." (Psalm 38:3, 7, 8, 10)

The priest, Zacharias, was in the temple burning incense, when Gabriel appeared to him and told him that he and Elisabeth would bear a son. (We know their son as John the Baptist.)

"And Zacharias said unto the angel, Whereby shall I know this? for I am an old man, and my wife well stricken in years. And the angel answering said unto him, I am Gabriel, that stand in the presence of God; and am sent to speak unto thee, and to shew thee these glad tidings. And, behold, **thou shalt be dumb, and not able to speak, until the day that these things shall be performed, because thou believest not my words**, which shall be fulfilled in their season." (Luke 1:18-20)

Zacharias was in the temple with Gabriel. The devil was not present. He was struck dumb by the Lord.

These Bible examples are just a few of many that show us that God often judges sin with sickness and even death. He uses sickness as a means of correction and discipline to bring His people to obedience.

"Let us search and try our ways, and turn again to the Lord. For the Lord will not cast off for ever: but though *he cause grief*, yet will he have compassion according to the multitude of his mercies. For he doth not afflict willingly nor grieve the children of men." (Lamentations 3:40 & 31-33)

Conclusion

God loves you. God also hates sin. If you have been involved in sin, it could be that your sickness is God's judgment or chastisement. There is only one thing you can do. God says, "If we confess our sins, he is faithful and just to forgive us our sins, and to cleanse us from all unrighteousness." (I John 1:9)

When we have repented to God and confessed our sins, God assures us, "Blessed is he whose transgression is forgiven, whose sin is covered." (Psalm 32:1)

God tells us how to prepare for a communion service: "Let a man examine himself ... he that eateth and drinketh unworthily, eateth and drinketh damnation to himself, not discerning the Lord's body. For this cause many are weak and *sickly* among you, and many sleep. For *if we would judge ourselves*, *we should not be judged*. But *when we are judged*, we are *chastened of the Lord*, that we should not be condemned with the world." (I Corinthians 11:28-32)

Examine Yourself

Is it sin that has caused your sickness?

If it is, confess (admit) it to God.

Repent of your sin.

Turn from it.

Remember Jesus' words to the lame man He healed, "**Sin no more** lest a worse thing come upon thee."

Jesus told a woman, who had been caught in the act of adultery: "Neither do I condemn thee: go, and **sin no more**." (John 8:11)

Remember Romans 6:1-2 & 12 & 23: "Shall we continue in sin, that grace may abound? God forbid ... *Let not sin therefore reign in your mortal body* ... for *the wages of sin is death*; but the gift of God is eternal life through Jesus Christ our Lord."

If you honestly do not know of an unconfessed sin that would cause God to judge or chastise you, read on. There are two more reasons for sickness!

Some are sick so God can receive glory through their miraculous healing! You may be one who is ***marked for a miracle* – FOR THE GLORY OF GOD!**

Reason 6

FOR THE GLORY OF GOD

Lazarus was one of Jesus' closest friends. John wrote that Jesus loved Lazarus and his two sisters, Mary and Martha. He often went to their home to visit with them.

The day Lazarus became sick, his sisters knew they had to notify Jesus, their Friend and the Healer. They sent a message: "Lord, behold, he whom thou lovest is sick."

When Jesus heard it, He told His disciples: "This sickness is not unto death, but **for the glory of God**, that **the Son of God might be glorified**." (John 11:3-4)

Then Jesus did a strange thing. He remained where He was, rather than rushing to His friend's bedside. After two days of seeming unconcerned, Jesus said to His disciples, "Let us go into Judaea again." Then He added, "Our friend Lazarus sleepeth; but I go, that I may awake him out of sleep."

His disciples answered, "Lord, if he sleep, he shall do well."

John then explained to us: "Howbeit Jesus spake of his death: but they thought that he had spoken of taking of rest in sleep. Then said Jesus unto them plainly, Lazarus is dead. And I am glad for your sakes that I was not there, to the intent *ye may believe* ... " (John 11:7 & 11-15)

When Jesus and His disciples finally arrived, Lazarus had already been buried for four days.

Both of his sisters ran to Jesus with identical greetings: "Lord, if thou hadst been here, my brother had not died!" (John 11:21 & 32)

Jesus walked with them and their friends to the grave site. He stood weeping at the tomb that held His friend. Then He ordered that the stone sealing the cave be rolled away.

Martha objected to His strange request.

She explained to Jesus that her brother had been dead for four days, and by this time his body had begun to decay. She said it in these words, "Lord, by this time he stinketh. Jesus saith unto her, Said I not unto thee, that, if thou wouldest believe, thou shouldest see the **GLORY OF GOD?**"

The stone was removed. Jesus then cried to His dead friend, "Lazarus, ***COME FORTH***!"

Lazarus lay cold and lifeless in his tomb. His body was wrapped tightly with grave clothes, and another cloth was wrapped around his face. But when Jesus Christ, the Son of the living God, the Creator of mankind, issued that command, **LIFE** stirred within Lazarus.

He came out of his tomb to meet His Master and His Friend. What a miracle the mourners saw that day! They must have stared in awe with both amazement and horror as Lazarus' tightly bound body floated from his grave and stood before them. They were obviously in shock, for it wasn't until Jesus told them to loose Lazarus and let him go, that they ran to his side and unwrapped him.

Then their eyes turned to the One who had issued the command. They realized that this humble Son of Man standing among them was no mere man. He was exactly who He claimed to be – the only begotten Son of the living God. – LIFE Himself!

John recorded the result of that miracle. "Then many of the Jews which came to Mary, and had seen the things which Jesus did, **believed on him**." (John 11:45)

The next time Jesus went to Lazarus' house, the town was still humming with the story of the miracle. "Much people of the Jews therefore knew that he was there: and they came not for Jesus' sake only, but that they might see Lazarus also, whom he had raised from the dead. But the chief priests consulted that they might put Lazarus also to death; because that **by reason of him** many of the Jews went away, and **believed on Jesus**." (John 12:9-11)

Prior to his resurrection, Lazarus had suffered for days with a sickness. His sisters probably hovered over him, praying for him, cooling his brow, feeding him broth, and watching intently for Jesus' arrival. He got worse, until he no longer even had the strength to take another breath.

Mary and Martha had been close to their brother. His unexpected death filled them with sorrow.

They notified their friends of his death, and many of them came to their home to weep with them.

But the pain Lazarus and his sisters endured for those few days was nothing, compared to the endless pain that souls without Christ will suffer throughout eternity.

Many people believed on Jesus, because they saw the

miracle of Lazarus' death and resurrection. *__Because of his pain, they were spared theirs.__*

Jesus loved Lazarus, but He also loved Lazarus' neighbors and friends, and was concerned about their eternal destiny. So He allowed Lazarus to suffer temporarily, so that others would not have to suffer eternally.

"This sickness ... is for *the glory of God.* By reason of (Lazarus) many of the Jews ... believed on Jesus."

__It was another day; another place; another man.__

As Jesus was going through a town, He stopped to touch a man who had been blind from birth.

His disciples asked Jesus: "Master, who did sin, this man, or his parents, that he was born blind? Jesus answered, *"Neither hath this man sinned, nor his parents*: but that *the works of God* should be made manifest in him."* (John 9:2-3)

Could it be that you are sick, so the works of God can be seen **in you**?

John also tells us that a great multitude followed Jesus, because they saw his miracles which he did on them that were diseased." (John 6:2)

The religious leaders of Jesus' day loved the favor and respect of the people. They held a council to discuss Jesus.

"What do we?" they questioned among themselves. "For this man doeth *many miracles*. If we let him thus alone, *all men will believe on him:* and the Romans shall come and take away both our place and our nation!" (John 11:47-48)

Peter described Jesus this way, in one of his sermons:

"Jesus of Nazareth, a man approved of God among you *by miracles and wonders and signs*, which God did by him in the midst of you." (Acts 2:22)

Jesus often taught that one's healing depended on his faith. "According to your faith be it unto you," He told the two blind men. (Matthew 9:29)

If there had been no sick people who had faith in the loving, miracle-working Son of the living God – who would He have healed?

Many people surrounded Jesus the day the woman, with an incurable disease, pressed through the crowd. Finally she came within reach of the hem of His robe. She could get no closer, so by faith in His healing power, she touched His garment. She was instantly healed. (See Mark 5:25-29.) The crowd that witnessed her miracle carried the news of her healing to their homes and villages. Others believed that if they could just touch the hem of His garment, they too could be healed.

Matthew tells us about the day that Jesus and His disciples entered the land of Gennesaret. "And when the men of that place had knowledge of him, they sent out into all that country round about, and brought unto him all that were diseased; and besought him that they might *only touch the hem of his garment*: and as many as touched were made perfectly whole." (Matthew 14:35-36)

Touching His hem began with one woman with faith. The miracle she received inspired others to believe for their miracles. It was *her sickness* that allowed her to *become a blessing* to others. Her story still inspires us today!

After the years Jesus spent walking among men, touching them, blessing them, healing them, and talking to them about His Father, He left earth and commissioned His followers to carry on His work, in His name.

Peter and John were two who followed His example. As they were going into the temple to pray, they were stopped by the pitiful cries of a crippled beggar, asking them for money.

Peter looked upon him, and compassion moved him to act. He said, "Silver and gold have I none; but such as I have give I thee: in the name of Jesus Christ of Nazareth rise up and walk. And he took him by the right hand, and lifted him up: and immediately his feet and ankle bones received strength. And he leaping up stood, and walked, and entered with them into the temple, walking, and leaping, and praising God. And all the people saw him walking and praising God:" (Acts 3:6-9)

Can you imagine the shock of the people who had passed by the beggar for years, and had often given him their change?

Peter preached to the crowd that had gathered. He told them about Jesus and His power to heal and save. As a result of the miracle and his sermon, he and John spent the night in jail.

But listen to the rest of the story . . .

"Howbeit many of them which heard the word believed; and the number of the men was about five-thousand!" (Acts 4:4)

Just one beggar – but he was **marked for a miracle**. He had spent his years suffering shame and pain, and was both scorned and helped by the healthy. He no doubt thought his life was of no value.

The days and years dragged by, with hopeless and helpless repetition. Nothing changed – until the day arrived that he was destined to receive his miracle.

He caused the entire city to come face to face with our miracle-working God, and five-thousand men were born into the kingdom of God, as a result of his miracle. His useless life and wasted years had meaning. He was a vessel, chosen by the Creator, to bring many people to salvation.

Philip also carried on the works of Christ. As he went to Samaria to evangelize, "the people with one accord gave heed unto those things which Philip spake, **hearing and seeing the miracles which he did**. For unclean spirits, crying with loud voice, came out of many that were possessed with them: and many taken with palsies, and that were lame, were healed. And there was great joy in that city." (Acts 8:6-8)

The disciples went in Jesus' name, "and preached every where, the Lord working with them, and **confirming the word with signs following**." (Mark 16:20)

The Jews were first given the gospel message. Then God expanded the field of evangelism, and sent Paul and Barnabas to the Gentiles.

They told the congregation of believers at Antioch that God had "opened the door of faith unto the Gentiles." (Acts 14:27)

At a later meeting in Jerusalem, they stood to speak. "Then all the multitude kept silence, and gave audience to Barnabas and Paul, declaring what *miracles and wonders* God had wrought among the Gentiles by them." (Acts 15:12)

Again, God used miracles to bring the Gentiles into His kingdom.

Paul later wrote: "How shall we escape, if we neglect so great salvation; which at the first began to be spoken by the Lord, and was confirmed unto us by them that heard him; God also bearing them witness, *both with signs and wonders, and with divers miracles*, and gifts of the Holy Ghost, according to his own will?" (Hebrews 2:3-4)

God confirmed His Word with signs, wonders, and miracles!

You may be one who is *marked for a miracle* that will bring glory to God. Your miracle may cause others to believe on Jesus Christ. Perhaps you have been witnessing of Christ's love to a friend, neighbor, or a family member for years.

Your sickness, followed by a miracle, may be what God will use to confirm His Word to others.

You *will* receive your miracle. Every child of God will one day be completely whole. All pain, tears, sorrow, disease, and sickness will be forever erased.

Martha realized this truth.

As Jesus was telling her that her brother, Lazarus, would rise again, she was standing by the grave of her deceased brother. She replied impatiently, "I know that he shall rise again in the resurrection at the last day!" (John 11:24)

She didn't yet realize that her brother was **marked for**

a miracle in this life. Martha had lost her faith in a miracle, the moment Lazarus took his last breath. She believed that the time for a miracle had passed.

She and Mary had probably often run to the window since they had summoned Jesus to Lazarus's bedside. But He had not come when they expected Him to come. And when He finally arrived, it was too late. Martha's faith for her brother's healing was gone. It had not happened while she was crying out for it. Now her brother lay in his tomb, where his lifeless body had been for four days. She had believed, but the miracle she had hoped for had not come. However, death itself could not prevent a miracle from taking place in Lazarus. Jesus had said that *He would be glorified through Lazarus* – and He was – at God's appointed time and place.

The woman who touched the hem of Jesus' garment had first suffered with the disease for twelve years. *Then her healing came*.

The man, who suffered for thirty-eight long years, may have lost hope for a miracle. Then Jesus suddenly arrived at the pool of Bethesda, and asked him, "Wilt thou be made whole?"

When he obeyed Jesus' commandment to take up his bed and walk, the paralysis, that had imprisoned his body, was instantly gone.

The blind man was no longer a child, but an adult, before he finally received his sight.

The beggar, who lay in front of the temple, may have heard Scriptures read, sermons preached, and songs sung. But he remained sick, until his day came for his miracle.

Don't lose faith in God! He is a Healer! There is a time set for your healing!

Ecclesiastes 3:1-8 tells us: "To every thing there is a season, and a time to every purpose under the heaven: a time to be born, and a time to die; a time to plant, and a time to pluck up that which is planted; a time to kill, and **a time to heal**; a time to break down, and a time to build up; a time to weep, and a time to laugh; a time to mourn, and a time to dance; a time to cast away stones, and a time to gather stones together; a time to embrace, and a time to refrain from embracing; a time to get, and a time to lose; a time to keep, and a time to cast away; a time to rend, and a time to sew; a time to keep silence, and a time to speak; a time to love, and a time to hate; a time of war, and a time of peace."

You may have sought the Lord to heal you. You may have had faith that you would receive your miracle. But you didn't. And you may have decided that you are destined to remain sick, and that you will not receive your miracle.

We remind you again that every single child of God will positively receive their healing. Heaven is our destination, and there will be no sickness in heaven. Those, who have not received their healing before the day that they are carried by the angels into heaven and ushered into the throne room, will stand whole before their Creator!

You may have resigned yourself to believe that your miracle will not occur before that day. Martha knew that Lazarus would one day be healed, but she lost her faith for a miracle in this life. When she asked Jesus for

His help, He did not answer her immediately. So she gave up.

Perhaps you have prayed that Jesus would touch you, but you have not yet received His reply. ***He has received your message!***

Psalm 34:15 promises us that "The eyes of the LORD are upon the righteous, and ***his ears are open unto their cry**.*"

"There is **a time to heal**." ***That time could be today**.*

You do not know God's time table. Your one responsibility is to keep your faith in the God who loves you enough to not only save you, but to heal you. Look forward to your healing! It will come – in God's time!

Some claim that the day of miracles is in the past. Yet they believe that they will one day defy the law of gravity and rise to meet their Savior in the air, when He returns to gather His people to Himself! And those who are alive and remain on earth will be part of that incredible miracle – and it is yet to come! The day of miracles is definitely not over!

When God called Moses to His service, Moses asked Him: "Behold, when I come unto the children of Israel, and shall say unto them, The God of your fathers hath sent me unto you; and they shall say to me, What is his name? what shall I say unto them? And God said unto Moses, **I Am That I Am**: and he said, Thus shalt thou say unto the children of Israel, **I Am** hath sent me unto you." (Exodus 3:13-14)

God did not tell Moses that His name is "**I WAS**."

He did not call Himself by the name, "**I WILL BE**."

He said His name is, and will forever be, "**I AM!**"

David wrote: "Bless the Lord, O my soul: and all that is within me, bless his holy name ... bless the Lord, O my soul, and forget not *all his benefits:* Who forgiveth all thine iniquities; who **healeth** all thy diseases."

"**I AM** the Lord that healeth thee," God told His people. (Exodus 15:26)

Jesus read in the synagogue: "The Spirit of the Lord is upon me, because he hath anointed me to preach the gospel to the poor; he hath sent me to *heal the broken-hearted*, to preach deliverance to the captives, and *recovering of sight to the blind*, to set at liberty them that are bruised, to preach the acceptable year of the Lord." (Luke 4:18-19)

Isaiah prophesied of Jesus: "But he was wounded for our transgressions, he was bruised for our iniquities: the chastisement of our peace was upon him; and **with his stripes we are healed**." (Isaiah 53:5)

Peter looked back upon that dark day when Jesus was beaten and nailed to the cross.

He wrote of his Savior and Healer: "Who his own self bare our sins in his own body on the tree, that we, being dead to sins, should live unto righteousness: **by whose stripes ye were healed**." (I Peter 2:24)

The Bible tells us that Jesus was not only nailed to the cross, but He was also scourged.

Men often died during a Roman scourging. They were first tied to a post. Then a soldier, whose arm bulged with rippling muscles, picked up a whip that had twelve strands of leather fastened to it. Pieces of sharp metal or bone were on each strand. As the soldier lashed the whip cruelly across the naked back of the accused, the strands often wrapped around to the front of the body. At times, the bowels were spilled out.

The whip tore across our Healer's back, not once or twice, but thirty-nine times. He was left so wounded, that He could not carry His heavy cross up Golgotha's hillside. Blood was pouring from His shredded back.

"...and by his stripes ye were healed."

The stripes were the cuts that Jesus received from the scourge.

Twelve strands of leather –
  Thirty-nine lashes –
    Four-hundred sixty-eight cuts –
      sliced the back of Jesus.

Don't ever believe the devil's lie that Jesus does not care about your sickness.

He told you to cast **all** your cares upon Him, for He cares for you.

He saw a blind man's need for a miracle, even when He was escaping men who wanted to stone Him.

He looked ahead in time to you, and saw your sickness, as He endured the whipping.

He took the beating – *for you*.

If your healing will bring **glory to God**, and He has marked you for a miracle, you will receive your healing - in *His time*.

God said of Himself, through His prophet, Malachi: "I am the Lord, *I change not*."

James 1:17 teaches us: "Every good gift and every perfect gift is from above, and cometh down from the

Father of lights, **with whom is no variableness, neither shadow of turning**."

Paul described Jesus as: "Jesus Christ the same yesterday, and **to day**, and for ever." (Hebrews 13:8)

The Jesus of yesterday is the Jesus of today!

Before Jesus finished His earthly walk and ascended to heaven, He made provisions for us to be healed in His name. He said: "And these signs shall follow *them that believe*; in my name shall they cast out devils ... *they shall lay hands on the sick, and they shall recover*." (Mark 16:17-18)

He did not say, as many teach today, that these signs would follow only His disciples. Neither did He say that these signs would only follow pastors and evangelists.

Jesus said, "These signs shall follow **THEM THAT BELIEVE!**"

There are still those today who believe that Christ works through His people who reach out with compassion to touch and pray for those with needs.

According to Christ's own words, as long as there are believers, there will be signs following them.

One of these signs is healing of the body, and there are multitudes of people who have testimonies of miraculous healings.

Don't be misled into believing only in the Jesus of the past. Jesus is present today, for His name is "**I AM**".

Conclusion

God's healing power still flows. Do you realize that you could be one who is marked for a miracle? Don't lose faith! Don't give up hope! If God urges you to ask a believer to pray for you, don't stiffen your neck and harden your heart! Don't say, "It would do me no good. I have been prayed for before, and I wasn't healed. God is not going to heal me. Why pray about it?"

Don't allow Satan, the liar and the thief, to steal your faith and your hope!

Be obedient to God's voice!

Keep your faith in His healing touch on your body, until the day it happens!

If you were not healed at the time you thought you would be, keep praising Him!

Never doubt that Jesus is the Healer! Realize that your miracle will come ... *in God's time* ... *in God's way*.

Examine Yourself

Have you, like Martha, lost hope in receiving the miracle that you have prayed for? Have you prayed for your miracle, but lost faith because it has not happened yet? Have you insisted that He heal you in *your* time, rather than in *His* time?

Confess to God that your faith in His love for you has wavered. Tell Him, from a sincere heart, that you are willing to be a vessel for Him to use, in whatever way He desires, at whatever time He thinks best, to bring others into His kingdom by your miracle.

There is nothing a Christian should desire more, than to bring glory to God!

Praise Him for the scourging He endured for your healing.

Thank Him for your healing that will surely come, in His appointed time.

"For I reckon that the sufferings of this present time are not worthy to be compared with the glory which shall be revealed in us." (Romans 8:18)

A PERSONAL TESTIMONY FROM CAROLYN

Paul and I were together in the doctor's office to hear the results of my test. He didn't soften the shocking news: "You have the worst case of cirrhosis of the liver I have ever seen."

He then asked how much alcohol I consumed a day. I replied that I didn't drink and never had. I went on to say that my favorite beverage is water. My husband confirmed this. A few minutes later, I was moved by a nurse to another room, this time without my husband present. I realized why later. The doctor questioned me again about my drinking habits, thinking I would then confess what I didn't want my husband to know. I assured him I was not a closet drinker! He didn't believe me, but he finally gave up trying to make me confess my out of control alcohol consumption. He instructed his nurse to make an appointment for me to discuss future treatment.

My husband and I visited a friend in the hospital. After praying for him, Paul stood by a window in the hospital, silently begging God to heal me. God answered. The Lord told him that he did not need to ask Him to heal me again. He had already done it!

Peace and thanksgiving filled me, when he told me about his prayer and God's answer. Paul is not one to lightly say, "God spoke to me." He is also not one who claims his will, rather than submitting to God's will.

When he said that God had spoken to him, I knew that He had. Jesus said, "My sheep hear my voice." (John 10:27)

I kept my appointment with the doctor. When he began to explain the seriousness of my disease and the only possible treatment to avoid death, I interrupted.

"I want another test before even thinking about treatment."

He was shocked.

"Why?"

"The Lord has healed me."

He stared. First, I refused to confess I was a drunk. Now I insisted that God had healed me.

"There is no need to get another test," he said emphatically. "The numbers will not come down by themselves."

"I know. I don't expect them to come down by themselves. The Lord has healed me of this disease, and He is the One who has brought them down. I do not want any discussion of treatment, until another test is taken."

He abruptly left the room.

Before I left his office, I was given an appointment to go to the lab to receive another test.

I knew what the results would be. The nurse called to tell me that I would not need to see the doctor again. I no longer had cirrhosis of the liver.

I didn't know the rest of the story until a few days later . . .

One of the doctor's nurses called me. She said, "I wanted to tell you why you had cirrhosis of the liver. We, who are Christians in this office, have been praying that the doctor would believe in God. We prayed that he would see a miracle. ***He saw one. Your healing was the answer to our prayers***."

I asked her what his response was.

She said that they have caught him studying my chart more than once.

I was one who was ***marked for a miracle – for the glory of God!***

Even if you have already received help and answers from the Scriptures quoted in this book, don't lay it down yet!

There is still help for you in the last chapter. For we ***all*** need to realize that - **GOD IS GOD**!

Reason 7

GOD IS GOD!

Our generation seems to have lost sight of the fact that *GOD IS GOD*!

Some have twisted and bent a few Scriptures and taught that God's people have the right to tell God what to do and how and when to do it.

"Command ye me," is a verse quoted often by some Bible teachers. (Read Isaiah 45:11 in context! For Isaiah 45:9 says: "Woe unto him that striveth with his Maker!")

God is called our Father in the Scriptures. Jesus told us to address Him as, "Our Father."

What father will allow his child to command and order him to fulfil his wishes?

"Dad, buy me a motorcycle right now! I demand one!"

Dad looks beyond his rebellious son's demand to his son's friends who are in the forming stages of an irresponsible gang.

"No, Son," he replies. "For your own good, you cannot have one."

"I order you to get me a bike! I command you!" the son yells.

Only an over-indulgent parent, who does not exercise his God-given authority over his child, would grant the child's request.

Even though the father realizes his son may become even more rebellious when he doesn't receive what he demands, a good father will do what is best for his son. When a parent gives a child everything he demands, the child will soon be the one in authority, and the parent will be under his control.

Many, who claim to be God's children, treat God in this manner, desiring to control Him.

"I command You!"

"I claim this, in Jesus' name. *Your will* does not matter to me. I want *my will* – and I want it *now*."

"Give me this desire of my heart. I demand it!"

God answers, "Ye ask, and receive not, because *ye ask amiss*, that ye may consume it upon your lusts. *Who is he that saith, and it cometh to pass, when the Lord commandeth it not*?" (James 4:3 and Lamentations 3:37)

When the heavens are silent, God's stubborn child becomes even more rebellious. He has learned from today's teachers that he can claim what he desires. And many lose faith in God's love for them, because they did not receive what they commanded Him to give.

Jesus was the beloved Son of God. As His Father watched His Son's baptism, love for His obedient Son overflowed from heaven to earth. God's voice echoed from the heavens: "This is my beloved Son, in whom I am well pleased." (Matthew 3:17)

But even this beloved Son did not get His way, as He pleaded with His Father to spare Him from giving His life on the cross.

He told His disciples in the Garden of Gethsemane: "My soul is exceeding sorrowful, even unto death: tarry ye here, and watch with me. And he went a little farther, and fell on his face, and prayed, saying, O my Father, if it be possible, let this cup pass from me: nevertheless **_not as I will, but as thou wilt_.**"

He returned to His sleeping disciples, then, "He went away again the second time, and prayed, saying, O my Father, if this cup may not pass away from me, except I drink it, **_thy will be done_**. And he came and found them asleep again: for their eyes were heavy. And he left them, and went away again, and **_prayed the third time, saying the same words_**." (Matthew 26:38-39 + 42-44)

His body lay spent, drenched with sweat. His Father dispatched an angel to minister to Him. But His Father did not change His plan for His Son's life. God's will did not change. Instead, Jesus submitted His will to His Father's plan of salvation.

During the earthly sojourn of Jesus, He walked on water - **_taking authority over the law of gravity_**.

He fed five-thousand hungry men and their families with a lad's lunch - **_taking authority over matter_**.

He called Lazarus from his grave - **_taking authority over death._**

He healed the sick - **_taking authority over disease._**

He set captives free - **_taking authority over devils._**

He calmed the sea - **_taking authority over the wind._**

But He never took authority over His Father.
Why would anyone today think that they could?

We are the bride of Christ. We are the sons and daughter of God. Neither relationship puts us in a position to command God to do for us what we demand of Him. It is time we recognize God for who He is.

HE IS GOD!

God's will was to prove Job. Job lay in the dust, pain overtaking him, and nearly consuming him.

He could have rebuked the devil.

The healing evangelists and prophets could have laid hands on him, rebuking his boils and poverty and praying a prayer of faith over his weakened body.

Job could have commanded God to heal him.

But all of it together would have done no good.

God had lowered the hedge around Job. Job was completely unaware of things that were happening in the heavens. God's purpose had to be accomplished.

Job had no knowledge of the conversation between God and Satan, concerning him. He had no idea why he was sick. Job had been chosen by God to be tested. He was singled out, because "there is none like him in the earth, a *perfect* and an **upright** man, one that *feareth God*, and *escheweth evil.*"

God said, "I have moved against him **without cause**."

Job could not – and did not – know why he was sick. What was happening to him was happening for one reason – **God's reason**.

Job had one responsibility through it all … simply to trust God, whatever came, until the test was over.

"Curse God and die!" his wife sighed bitterly. She was one who wanted God under her control. If God did not give Job what she wanted Him to give, then curse Him.

Would you yield to your child's demands, if he attempted to control you?

Or would you teach him, by not giving him his way,

that he is the child, and you are the parent?

Would you teach him the proper way to ask, by withholding your favors from him, until he learned how to approach you respectfully with his requests?

A sickness can sometimes be our Father's megaphone to get our attention, so He can make us a better child!

Even though God has freely given us salvation through the shed blood of His only begotten Son, He wants us to come before Him, with a broken and humble heart, *asking* for mercy, not *demanding* it.

Jesus commended the sinner, who stood in the temple and smote himself upon his breast, and cried humbly: "God be merciful to me a sinner." (Luke 18:13)

The same is true for the one who approaches God to ask for healing. The price has been paid, but God wants us to come *asking* for His mercy, rather than *demanding* His healing touch.

No one ever approached Jesus as He walked this earth, and commanded Him to heal him.

The blind men cried, "Thou Son of David, *have mercy* on us!"

The woman, with the issue of blood, merely crept to His side, and reached out and touched the hem of His garment.

The Canaanite woman came worshiping Him, begging for the healing of her daughter. She compared herself to a dog eating the crumbs that had fallen from its master's table.

The father, who had the devil possessed son, knelt before Jesus, saying, "Lord, *have mercy* on my son."

Jairus fell at the feet of Jesus and besought Him

greatly to heal his daughter.

Even the man we refer to as Legion, ran and worshiped Jesus when he saw Him. (Mark 5:6)

The Scriptures do not tell us of one person who demanded healing of Jesus.

God counsels His children, "In every thing by prayer and supplication with thanksgiving let your *requests* be made known unto God." (Philippians 4:6)

Let your *requests* - not your demands - be known to God.

"God, why am I sick?" Perhaps your prayers for healing have not been answered, because God wants you to learn that there is a proper way and a right attitude in which to approach Him.

God said to Job: "Shall he that contendeth with the Almighty instruct him? he that reproveth God, let him answer it."

Job replied in a voice grown small: "Behold, I am vile; what shall I answer thee? *I will lay mine hand upon my mouth*. Once have I spoken; but I will not answer: yea, twice; but *I will proceed no further*." (Job 40:2 & 4-5)

There are many today who have approached God in an obnoxious and arrogant way. Perhaps many, like Job, should lay their hands upon their mouths.

Some argue, "But God says to approach His throne of grace boldly!" If we realized who this great God is, we would also realize that we must have boldness to approach His throne at all.

Isaiah described the God, who scoops up the Atlantic, Pacific, and Indian oceans, the Baltic and Red seas, the Nile and Euphrates rivers, the Great Lakes, and all the other large and small bodies of water on our planet - and cups them in the hollow of His hand! (Isaiah 40:12)

Man believes that he has conquered the universe, because he succeeded in sending men to the moon. But God measures the heavens beyond the moon, beyond the planets and our galaxy, out into multitudes of other galaxies, as yet undiscovered and unnamed by man – all with His arm's span! (See Isaiah 40:12.) The higher man reaches with his powerful telescopes, the more vast he realizes the heavens are. Until February 26, 2014, man believed that there were 1,000 planets in our galaxy. However, on that day, they discovered 715 more planets! In the galaxy of our sun, scientists estimate that there are over 100 thousand million stars! Astronomers now tell us that there are millions upon millions of other galaxies and as many as 300 sextillion stars. (One sextillion is 1,000,000,000,000,000,000,000!) How big is God? It only takes the span of His arm to include them all.

God heaps all the dust of the earth in His measuring cup, as easily as a baker measures flour for a cake! (Isaiah 40:12)

God picks up the Andes, Blue Ridge, Alps, Smoky Mountain, and Appalachian ranges, along with all the rest of earth's lofty mountains and hills – and places them on His balancing scale. (Isaiah 40:12)

He looks at the great nations of this age, the United States of America, China, Russia, and all the other lands man has separated into nations. And He compares their sum to one drop of water in a bucket or to one speck of dust on a balance.

He adds up the Hawaiian, Caribbean, Faukland, and Philippine Islands, mixes them together with Australia and all the other lands situated in bodies of waters – and dismisses their sum as a very little thing. (Isaiah 40:15)

Isaiah graphically paints this picture of God: "To whom will ye liken God? or what likeness will ye compare unto him? It is he that sitteth upon the circle of the earth, and **the inhabitants thereof are as grasshoppers**; that **stretcheth out the heavens as a curtain, and spreadeth them out as a tent** to dwell in." (Isaiah 40:18 & 22)

Daniel tells us that King Nebuchadnezzar learned this important truth: "And all the inhabitants of the earth are reputed as nothing: and he doeth according to **his will** in the army of heaven, and among the inhabitants of the earth: and none can stay his hand, or say unto him, What doest thou?" (Daniel 4:35)

God said to Isaiah: "Understand that I am he: before me there was no God formed, neither shall there be after me. I, even I, am the Lord; and beside me there is no saviour." (Isaiah 43:10-11)

The princes and judges, who hold power over the lives of billions of men, are as nothing to God. In fact, Isaiah says God will merely blow upon them – not step upon them or swat them – but just blow upon them, and these feared leaders will "wither, and the whirlwind shall take them away as stubble." (Isaiah 40:24)

When God descended to Mount Sinai to speak to His people, the mountain trembled. The deafening sound of a trumpet blast rent the air. Mothers clutched their children tightly, for they had all been warned that whoever even touched the mountain would instantly die. The Israelites stared wide-eyed, as God descended upon that trembling mountain in a fire, and smoke belched from it, as from a mighty furnace.

The people cried to Moses: "Speak thou with us, and we will hear: but let not God speak with us, lest we die." (Exodus 20:19)

That God of yesterday is the same God we so flippantly approach today.

After Paul told us to come boldly before God's throne, he added: "For ye are not come unto the mount that might be touched, and that burned with fire, nor unto blackness, and darkness, and tempest, and the sound of a trumpet, and the voice of words; which voice they that heard intreated that the word should not be spoken to them any more: (for they could not endure that which was commanded, and if so much as a beast touch the mountain, it shall be stoned, or thrust through with a dart: and so terrible was the sight, that Moses said, I exceedingly fear and quake:)

"But ye are come unto mount Sion, and unto the city of the living God, the heavenly Jerusalem, and to an innumerable company of angels, to the general assembly and church of the firstborn, which are written in heaven, and to God the Judge of all, and to the spirits of just men made perfect, and to Jesus the mediator of the new covenant, and to the blood of sprinkling, that speaketh better things than that of Abel. See that ye refuse not him that speaketh. For if they escaped not who refused him that spake on earth, much more shall not we escape, if we turn away from him that speaketh from heaven: whose voice then shook the earth: but now he hath promised, saying, Yet once more I shake not the earth only, but also heaven. And this word, Yet once more, signifieth the removing of those things that are shaken, as of things that are made, that those things which cannot be shaken may remain.

"Wherefore we receiving a kingdom which cannot be moved, let us have grace, whereby we may serve God acceptably with *reverence* and *godly fear:* for **our God is a consuming fire.**" (Hebrews 12:18-29)

"Come <u>boldly</u> unto the throne of grace ..." (Hebrews 4:16)

Walk into the throne room, where over one-hundred million angels are gathered around their Creator, worshiping and praising Him. (See Revelation 5:11.)

Move through the midst of all the spirits of those made perfect by the blood of Jesus.

Glance in awe at the cherubims. (Ezekiel 10:1)

Hear the seraphims, reverently chanting: "Holy, holy, holy is the Lord of hosts." (Isaiah 6:2-3)

But the most astounding sight of all is the throne of God. As you move toward it, the brightness of God suddenly enfolds you. Colors explode around you.

You feel as if you are standing within a rainbow! (Revelation 4:3)

You are there – standing before your God. Lift your eyes to look upon the One seated on the throne. His shining garment glistens as sunlit snow. (Daniel 7:9)

A fiery stream issues from before Him. (Daniel 7:10)

Your eyes are finally drawn to His face. There is only one way to even attempt to describe it. It is as if you are looking into the sun. (Revelation 1:16)

Then you look at His eyes. They are like no eyes you have seen. They are as flames of fire. (Revelation 1:14)

Then He speaks to you. His voice reverberates through you. It can only be described as the rushing sound of many waters. (Revelation 1:15)

Isaiah looked upon this God, and cried, "Woe is me! for I am undone; because I am a man of unclean lips, and I dwell in the midst of a people of unclean lips: for mine eyes have seen the King, the Lord of hosts!" (Isaiah 6:5)

This is the God we approach with our requests! Yes, we are invited to approach Him boldly – not flippantly or informing Him what He is supposed to do and how and when He is to do our will.

We are told to approach Him with reverence and godly fear. We are told to enter into His gates with thanksgiving, into His courts with praise, and to come before His presence with singing. (Psalm 100:2 & 4)

Our generation of Christians desperately needs to be taught two simple facts that somehow today's church has lost sight of:

1. **GOD IS GOD.**
2. **MAN IS MAN.**

Don't try to put God in a box, and tell Him what He must do!

Don't be so foolish as to try to force God to conform to **your** will! Conform to **His** will! Trust Him! He knows the future! You don't!

Let Him have His way in your life and accomplish His will **in** and **through** you!

As Isaiah fell before God, he heard God ask, "Whom shall I send, and who will go for us?"

Isaiah answered, "Here am I; send me." (Isaiah 6:8)

God then sent him forth with this one command: "Go."

Before man goes out into the world, bearing the name of the Lord, he should first catch a glimpse of God's power and beauty and majesty and strength! He will then go into the world with unwavering faith.

He will then serve God acceptably with reverence and godly fear. He will then be able to teach others how to approach and serve this great God!

Trust God to work through you, in **His** way. Trust Him to do **His** will.

God has always worked in different ways in His people. His ways cannot be stereotyped. What He has done in and for others, He may not do for you!

There will be many things that you will not understand. Things happened in the lives of men in the Bible that we cannot understand.

"For my thoughts are not your thoughts, neither are your ways my ways, saith the Lord. For as the heavens are higher than the earth, so are my ways higher than your ways, and my thoughts than your thoughts." (Isaiah 55:8-9)

The great prophet of miracles, Elisha, had raised the dead – yet he died of a sickness. His corpse lay entombed in a sepulcher. A battle took place nearby, and a soldier was killed. As his comrades were burying him, their enemy again approached them. They didn't have time for a proper burial, so they threw his corpse into the sepulcher, where Elisha was buried. When the soldier's lifeless body touched Elisha's bones, he was instantly raised from the dead.

And yet, Elisha himself died of a sickness! (See II Kings 13:14 & 20-21.)

Why did Paul, used by God to do great miracles, tell Timothy: "Use a little wine for thy stomach's sake and thine often infirmities?"

Should we judge Timothy and Paul for their lack of faith? Paul was confident that Timothy was a man of God. He told the Philippians: "I trust the Lord Jesus to send Timotheus shortly unto you ... for *I have no man likeminded*, who will naturally care for your state."

Paul wrote to Timothy: "Trophimus have I left at Miletum sick." Why did Paul leave him behind, rather than commanding God to heal him?

Many times a loved one dies, and we don't understand. But perhaps God is preventing him from enduring a tragedy that would have befallen him, had he lived.

Isaiah 57:1-2 says: "The righteous perisheth, and no man layeth it to heart: and merciful men are taken away, none considering that the righteous is **_taken away from the evil to come_**. He shall enter into peace ..."

We may not understand things that happen to ourselves and to others. Our responsibility is not to understand, but to submit to God and trust Him.

For God **is** – and **always will be** – **GOD**!

Conclusion

Your prayers for God's healing touch may have been hindered by the attitude in which you have approached God.

He is to be approached with reverence.

Your *requests* – not your demands – are to be offered to Him, with a thankful heart for all the blessings He has already given you.

Examine Yourself

Have you approached God rebelliously – and even accusingly? Have you been unthankful for the blessings He has already showered upon you?

Or have you had an awed reverence, as you entered His throne room?

Have you **asked** Him for healing?

Or have you **commanded** Him to heal you?

If you have approached Him in such a way, go before Him again – this time with humility.

The prophet, Micah, counsels us, "He hath shewed thee, O man, what is good; and what doth the Lord require of thee, but to do justly, and to love mercy, and to **walk humbly with thy God**?" (Micah 6:8)

David wrote: "The sacrifices of God are a broken spirit: a **broken and a contrite heart**, O God, thou wilt not despise." (Psalm 51:17)

II Corinthians 7:1 tells us to "cleanse ourselves from all filthiness of the flesh *and spirit*, perfecting holiness in the fear of God."

Come before God with a thankful heart.

Praise Him for blessing you with salvation, forgiveness, cleansing, mercy, grace, and love.

Thank Him for your brothers and sisters in the Lord.

If you can, kneel before Him, or fall upon your face, and worship Him, as Jesus did in the Garden of Gethsemane.

Wait before God. Look at His majesty and His mighty power.

Ask Him for His healing touch. Wrap your request in thanksgiving and praise.

For **GOD IS GOD**.

Mediate upon Him. Look upon Him with spiritual eyes. Listen for His voice with spiritual ears.

Obey His commandment to ... **"Be still, and know that I am God**." (Psalm 46:10)

A FINAL WORD

𝔜ou are the only *you* that there is. You are a distinct individual – unique – one of a kind.

God knows you, not as just one tiny portion of the human race, but as **YOU**. We are told that the coded instructions contained in the DNA of just one of your cells would fill 4,000 encyclopedia sized books with meaningful information! Just one gram (0.022 lb) of your DNA can hold as much information as one trillion CDs!

Your Creator knows all there is to know about you. In fact, He knows more about you, than you know about yourself! Do you keep a running total of the number of hairs on your head? God does! He knows your thoughts. He knows your weaknesses, your faults, your hidden fears. And He loves you, as no one else can.

He created you for His pleasure.

He asks for your love in return.

Before Adam and Eve yielded to temptation, God walked in the Garden of Eden to visit with them every day. God was grieved when His fellowship with man was broken through sin.

He then sent Jesus to restore fellowship between God and man, for He desires this same close fellowship with you. Jesus became the sinless Mediator between God and man.

"For there is one God, and one mediator between God and men, the man Christ Jesus." (I Timothy 2:5)

God has not placed you in a file with a label on it. He has not categorized you.

People may label you, Poor, Rich, Black, White, Jew, Gentile, Protestant, Catholic – **but God doesn't.**

God sees you as … **you.** God will deal with you in a way that is just right for you. He healed the sick in different ways.

The Bible records only one time that a man was healed by dipping seven times in a river. That was the way God chose to heal Naaman of leprosy. Other lepers could have dipped seven times a day for seven years in the Jordan River, but it would have done them no good.

When King Hezekiah became deathly ill, God sent Isaiah to him with a message. He was to place a lump of figs on his boil. He did, and he was healed.

All the figs in the world will not heal another boil, unless it is God's will to move again in this way. The figs did not heal Hezekiah. Obedience to God's Word, no matter how foolish it seemed to the king, healed his boil.

Elisha was called to the bedside of a dead child. Elisha stretched himself out upon that lad's cold body, and prayed until the warmth of life entered him. Elisha then arose, and paced the floor. Then he again stretched himself out upon the boy. The boy sneezed seven times, opened his eyes, and life was restored. But will all dead boys be resurrected in this way? No! It was God's way of dealing through one prophet to raise one small lad.

One blind man's sight was restored, when Jesus spat onto the dirt, made clay, and spread it upon his eyes. He then sent him to wash it off. To our knowledge, Jesus never again used spittle and dirt to heal the blind.

God brought healing to some, as the disciples of Jesus anointed them with oil. He brought healing to others, as they laid their hands upon them. He touched others, as they just spoke the word, and empowered it with the name of Jesus.

Some were healed, as they stepped into Peter's shadow on a sunny day. Some were healed, as they laid a handkerchief or apron, that had been prayed over by Paul, on their diseased bodies.

Some miracles happened, when an angel descended upon the Pool of Bethesda and troubled the waters, and the sick got in the pool. Other miracles took place, as the sick inched their way through a crowd, and touched the hem of Jesus' garment.

The Bible tells us that Jesus ministered healing to all who were brought to Him in some cities.

Yet when He came to His own country, Mark wrote: "And he could there do no mighty work, save that he laid his hands upon a few sick folk, and healed them. And he marvelled because of their unbelief." (Mark 6:5-6)

Matthew also wrote of that time: "And he did not many mighty works there because of their unbelief." (Matthew 13:58)

Some churches will not see many miracles, because faith in a miracle-working God for our day is neither believed nor taught.

Do not doubt God, as the children of Israel doubted, during their time in the wilderness. The Bible tells us that they provoked and grieved God, because they *"limited the Holy One* of Israel." (Psalm 78:41)

Do not limit God's power to work a miracle in your life. His name is still **I AM**. Do not limit God to a time, a place, or a way to perform your healing.

Mary, the mother of Jesus, gave good advice, as mothers usually do. She spoke of her Son, Jesus, as she instructed the servants at the marriage feast:

"Whatsoever he saith unto you, do it."

We can still heed her words today.

Listen to the Lord's personal instructions to you. And when you hear His voice, obey Him. Again, we remind you of Mary's counsel: "*Whatsoever he saith unto you, do it*." (John 2:5)

We have discussed seven reasons why people get sick. Whatever the reason for your sickness, our God's words ring down through the ages, and they are forever true:

"I AM THE LORD THAT HEALETH THEE."

I. If the reason you are sick is for God to get your attention – then look upon Him! Receive Jesus Christ as your Savior and Lord. *Turn to Him for salvation, and be healed.*

Jesus told the man with the palsy, "Son, thy sins be forgiven thee."

Then He turned to the critical bystanders, and asked them: "Whether is it easier to say to the sick of the palsy, thy sins be forgiven thee; or to say, arise, and take up thy bed and walk?" (Mark 2:5 & 9)

If you are sick because God wants you to come to Him, then you do not have to stay sick. Paul did not stay blind! Naaman did not remain a leper! Nebuchadnezzar did not stay insane!

They were all healed - **when they turned to God! The greatest healing of all is your spiritual healing from the deadly disease of sin!**

II. If you are being tested and your faith has been severely tried, as Job's was, then hold onto your faith until God's will is accomplished in you, and you have endured the trial of your faith. *Keep trusting the Lord! Endure your test! Keep the faith – and be healed!*

III. If you are sick, so that God can mold you into a compassionate, effective witness of His grace, then minister to others – *just as you are and right where you are* – even as you wait on God for your own healing.

IV. If your sickness has been caused by an attack of the devil, then **submit your life to God, resist the devil** in the name of Jesus - and be healed.

V. If the reason you have been sick is because of sin in your life, then repent of your sins, and follow God's remedy for healing, just as explicitly as you expect a pharmacist to follow a doctor's order for a prescription.

God's written order is: "Is any sick among you? let him call for the elders of the church; and let them pray over him, anointing him with oil in the name of the Lord: and the prayer of faith shall save the sick, and the Lord shall raise him up; and *if he have committed sins, they shall be forgiven him.* Confess your faults one to another, and pray one for another, that ye may be healed. The effectual fervent prayer of a righteous man availeth much." (James 5:14-16)

VI. If you are sick because God has marked you for a miracle that He might receive glory, then wait on Him for your miracle. *Hold onto your faith* in God's love and healing power – and be healed!

VII. If you are sick so God can teach you that He is God, then consider His power and majesty. Go humbly before Him, with fear and reverence, and a spirit of thanksgiving. Let your requests – not your demands – be known to Him. Have confidence that God knows, even better than you do, what is best for your life. Let Him mold you into His image, in whatever way He chooses to do it. You will be healed – in *His* time – in *His* way!

It is little wonder that God promises that there will be no sorrow, crying, or pain in heaven.

There will be no reason for sickness in heaven!

- The saved will already be saved!
- The proving times will be over!
- Ministering comfort to one another will no longer be necessary!
- The devil will be locked in a bottomless pit forever, and can attack no more!

- There is no sin in heaven!
- All of heaven will be filled with the glory of God! No miracle could add to it!
- All creatures will know that God is GOD! Every knee will have bowed before Him!

Until that blessed day, do all that you can do, to prepare to receive your miracle. Then simply trust Him, and wait upon God for His appointed time to touch and heal you.

Who would have thought that Job, a broken, childless, grieving, destitute man, sitting in ashes, scraping his infested, running boils, would one day be the wealthy, healthy father of seven sons and three beautiful daughters, and would live on this earth for another 140 years and throughout eternity?

Who would have thought that Lazarus, entombed, enveloped in shrouds, and shut within a cave, would burst forth from his grave and shock his mourners?

Who would have thought, on that darkest of all days, when a cross stood silhouetted on Calvary's hill, and the life flowed from Jesus' tortured body, that one day He would descend from the heavens with a glorious shout, to claim His bride that He loves and redeemed with His own blood? "Even so, come, Lord Jesus!"

"Let us **hold fast the profession of our faith without wavering**; (for he is faithful that promised;) but without faith it is impossible to please him: for he that cometh to God must believe that he is, and that he is a rewarder of them that diligently seek him." (Hebrews 10:23 and 11:6)

"It is of the Lord's mercies that we are not consumed, because his compassions fail not. They are new every morning: great is thy faithfulness. The Lord is my portion, saith my soul; therefore will I hope in him. The Lord is good unto them that wait for him, to the soul that seeketh him. It is good that a man should both hope and quietly wait for the salvation of the Lord." (Lamentations 3:22-26)

"For thou, Lord, art good, and ready to forgive; and plenteous in mercy unto all them that call upon thee. Like as a father pitieth his children, so the Lord pitieth them that fear him. For he knoweth our frame; he remembereth that we are dust. But thou, O Lord, art a God full of compassion, and gracious, long suffering, and plenteous in mercy and truth."
PSALM 86:5 AND 103:13-14 AND 86:15

"O love the Lord, all ye his saints: for the Lord preserveth the faithful. Be of good courage, and he shall strengthen your heart, all ye that hope in the Lord." PSALM 31:23-24

"But unto you that fear my name shall the Sun of righteousness arise with healing in his wings." MALACHI 4:2

"Heal me, O Lord, and I shall be healed; save me, and I shall be saved: for *thou art my praise.*" JEREMIAH 17:14

I Never Forsake My Own

I am with you, My Child,
I am holding your hand.
For I never forsake My own.
In the blackest of the night,
I am your guiding Light.
No, I never leave My children alone.

I was with My prophet in a whale,
My disciples in a jail.
I have never forsaken My own.
Walked in fire with My three men,
Spent the night in a lion's den,
I have never left one child alone.

I'm with the sparrow when it falls,
I'm behind prison walls.
I am with you each moment of each day.
In the valley, down so low,
I'm the Lily there, you know,
I am with you each step of your way.

When you're sunk in deep despair,
Cast on Me your every care,
For I surround you with My love.
When you breathe your last breath,
I'll take you through the valley of death,
Then bring you to My home up above.

CAROLYN WILDE

WE'VE COME THIS FAR BY FAITH
BY CAROLYN WILDE

"I couldn't put this book down!" is the comment heard most often from readers of this inspiring book.

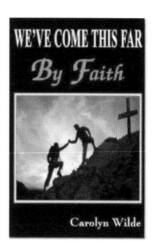

As he lay injured in an ambulance beside his bleeding daughter, Paul Wilde made a promise to God. It was a life-changing commitment that led Paul, Carolyn and their eight children into an extraordinary, living-by-faith adventure.

We've Come This Far by Faith will challenge and inspire you. This book is more than a heartwarming story about the faith journey of a family of ten who learned to trust God. The real story is about our living, faithful, loving God, who loves each of His children and cares about every single one of their needs!

We've Come This Far by Faith is full of thrilling answers to simple prayers - a loaf of bread when a family is gathered around the breakfast table; a van full of groceries pulling up when cupboards are empty and no one but God has been told there is a desperate need; a mysterious one word message ("Gas") to one of God's listening servants; an anonymous gift of over $220,000 to pay off a church mortgage - all in answer to prayer alone!

We've Come This Far by Faith will dare you and encourage you to trust God to guide you. The Christian life for every Christian should be an exhilarating faith adventure. We serve a real God who is anxious to take care of us and provide for every single one of our needs!

This is a book that will build your faith at this critical time in our unstable world. Each of us may soon be facing desperate needs. Each one of us needs to know that we can rely on God to provide our daily necessities!

We've Come This Far By Faith will help you to know that the God of the Bible is still the God of today!

We've Come This Far By Faith
Soft Cover – 286 Pages

TORCHBEARERS
By Carolyn Wilde

Dave, an Olympic champion runner, is called by Christ to run with the torch through this sin-blackened world. His race takes him into cities, prisons, skid row missions, campuses, lively churches, dead churches, and city parks. He meets skeptics, invalids, prisoners, alcoholics, homeless children, hardened juveniles, and two very different women.

His look backward through the past 2,000 years brings him face-to-face with valiant runners carrying the torch in every country.

He is shocked to discover:

- Augustine's concern about abortion – in the 5th century!
- Columba's raging temper that littered a field with 5,000 corpses!
- A woman and six men set aflame - for daring to teach their children the Lord's Prayer and Ten Commandments in the English language!

Dave is inspired by:

- John Hus, singing praises to God, while flames devour his body.
- Count Zinzendorf's around-the-clock, 100 year prayer meeting!

- Entire villages of American Indians praying and singing the night through!
- The thrilling conversion of young John Newton, the blasphemous slave trader.
- The near invalid, who made her way into Tibet by climbing treacherous mountains in raging blizzards – with a murderer as her guide!
- The young man who tapped into the storehouse of God, and became a loving Dad to over 9,500 orphans!

Be challenged along with Dave, as you read actual words from torchbearers' lips, prayers from their hearts, and, in some cases, their dying messages, meticulously gleaned from historical records.

Polycarp, Augustine, Patrick, Wyclif, Luther, Tyndale, Wesley, and Finney are all here. Some of the others you will meet are Columba, Waldo, Francke, Annie, Elizabeth, and Savonarola. Our rich Christian heritage will come alive, not just as historical figures, but as real men, women, teenagers, and children who overcame this world, their flesh, and the devil, by the blood of the Lamb, the word of their testimony, and their willingness to both live and die victoriously for their Lord.

Torchbearers is not just another novel with its fictional Dave.

Torchbearers is not just another history book with its nearly 40 biographies.

Torchbearers is a call. For it is high-time for all of us to run with the torch. And the race is not easy today. But then ... *it never has been*.

COMMENTS FROM READERS

"One of the best books I have ever read in my lifetime. My life and ministry have not been the same." DWIGHT L. KINMAN, AUTHOR, HOSPITAL CHAPLAIN & CONFERENCE SPEAKER

"I have shared many passages from **Torchbearers** with my friends and family. I could not put it down! I recommend this book to any person carrying the torch for Jesus who has ever felt alone, rejected, or just in need of a little encouragement." ROSEY BRYAN, WIFE OF ANDY, SOUTHERN BAPTIST EVANGELIST

"... a challenging message and a sharply painted picture of our rich Christian heritage." GULF COAST CHRISTIAN NEWSPAPER

"I was totally in awe! The encouragement one can receive from reading this book is much needed." QUINTON MILLS, EVANGELIST, SONGWRITER

"I constantly use portions of **Torchbearers,** as I minister to the Youth Group in our church." SUZANNE COURTRIGHT, TEEN TEACHER

TORCHBEARERS - Through Every Century

70 to 156 . . . . Polycarp

Died in 258 . . . . Lawrence

316 to 397 . . . . Martin of Tours

354 to 430 . . . . Augustine

The 400s . . . . Patrick

521 to 597 . . . . Columba

540 to 604 . . . . Gregory the Great

675 to 754 . . . . Boniface

801 to 865 . . . . Anskar

Died in 997 . . . . Adalbert

Died in 1012 . . . . . . Alphage

Died in 1045 . . . . . . Gerard

Died in 1079 . . . . . . Stanislaus

Late 1100s - 1217 . . Waldo

1334 to 1384 . . . . . . John Wyclif

1372 to 1415 . . . . . . John Hus

1452 to 1498 . . . . . . Girolamo Savonarola

1483 to 1547 . . . . . . Martin Luther

1494 to 1536 . . . . . . William Tyndale

1663 to 1727 . . . . . . August Francke

1669 to 1742 . . . . . . Susanna Wesley

1700 to 1760 . . . . . . Count Zinzendorf

1703 to 1791 . . . . . . John Wesley

1718 to 1747 . . . . . . David Brainerd

1725 to 1807 . . . . . . John Newton

1780 to 1845 . . . . . . Elizabeth Fry

1789 to 1871 . . . . . . Charlotte Elliott

1792 to 1875 . . . . . . Charles Finney

1805 to 1898 . . . . . . George Mueller

Born in 1855 . . . . . . Annie Taylor
1902 to 1970 . . . . . . Gladys Aylward
Running in 1920s . . Aged Woman
1910 to 1975 . . . . . . James Stewart
Today . . . . Dave

Torchbearers
Soft Cover: 432 Pages

A TALE OF TWO COUSINS

By Carolyn Wilde

A gripping allegory of Christ and His bride. You will meet two cousins, whose striking similarities contrast their deadly differences.

This unforgettable story will absorb you right up to the end. The best (or worst) part of this book is that you will meet yourself in many of its 297 pages.

READER'S COMMENTS

"I have read various expositions of Christ and His wonderful truths. This is truly one of the most Spirit-filled books that I have ever read. My life has been furthered in my spiritual growth as a child of God. It is a gift to the body of Christ. I use much of it in my preaching!" ANGEL SUAREZ, TACOMA, WASHINGTON

"This is the most unusual, moving book I have ever read. Stay with this book and this book will stay with you." BOB HARRINGTON, CSA (CERTIFIED SOUL WINNER)

"What a wonderful experience! I loved the story of Joe and Luke! I loved Part 2! Part 3 enthralled me! The way this story is woven with Scriptures is amazing!" GENE CALLAHAN

"This book held me captive from the first to the last page." BEVERLY WALKER

"I cried. I praised. I repented. I felt God's anointing as I read this inspired book. It is truly a call to end day saints!" SUZANNE COURTRIGHT

"I believe you intended the book for the unsaved, but I think it is so fitting for the church: the ones who have forgotten that this life is not all there is and that wrong will be made right when Christ returns. It is absolutely tremendous!" KARL CRAWFORD

"I found myself so many, many times in these pages. The journey of the Christian's walk came to life! I wept as I felt the love of the Groom for His beloved Bride. **A Tale of Two Cousins** will touch the hearts of the young and the old, the new and the mature Christian." ELIZABETH WALKER

A Tale of Two Cousins
Soft Cover: 297 Pages

SMITTEN SHEPHERDS

By Paul and Carolyn Wilde

18,000 pastors are leaving the ministry each year. That is *1,500 every single month*.

What is behind this exodus from the ministry?

Why are so many pastors burned out, emotionally fatigued, physically exhausted, and spiritually discouraged?

Smitten Shepherds is a book that is dedicated to pastors. It is to the point, straight from the heart and forged from our 30 plus years of pastoring. It is a book written, not to discourage, but to encourage. Pastors and their wives who have read this book are calling and writing to say they have been given extra strength for their race after reading "Smitten Shepherds". One evangelist ordered 100 to encourage pastors. Denominations are ordering 500 and 1,000 books at a time for pastors in their churches.

Pastoring today is harder than it was yesterday. It will be harder tomorrow than it is today. Will you be one of the 18,000 who walk away from the church, or will you be one who continues to fight the fight, keep the faith and finish your course?

These **122 pages** may make the difference.

Comments from Readers

"From page one, I was gripped, and could not put it down. I believe every minister and every minister's wife should read it, because, although following God's call is immensely rewarding, there are definite pitfalls we must avoid. Finally, we have a book that biblically and effectively addresses the very real challenges we face in the ministry. As a minister, we go through great challenges to our faith, family, and ministry. But, praise God, we can and will make it by the grace of God - just know that this book is a provision of His grace." *MIKE CROSLOW, EXECUTIVE DIRECTOR OF HARVEST CHURCHES INTERNATIONAL*

"This book is full of truth and it is strength for those not to give up their position in Christ as they serve the Lord in ministry and leadership. I am passing it on to the pastors on the campus." *Catherine Logan, President of Mount Zion School of Ministry*

Congregations: each of you need a copy too! Become one who lightens your pastor's load, rather than adding to it!

Smitten Shepherds
Soft Cover 122 Pages
(Call or write for a quantity price)

Made in the USA
Middletown, DE
21 September 2019